SHADOW CHILDREN

SHADOW CHILDREN

Understanding Education's #1 Problem

Anthony Dallmann-Jones, Ph.D.

Professor, Educational Studies Division, Marian College
Director, National At-Risk Education Network (NAREN)

◆RLD PUBLICATIONS, INC.

LANCASTER, PA

Shadow Children

RLD Publications, Inc.
1148 Elizabeth Avenue
Lancaster, Pennsylvania 17601 U.S.A.

Printed in the United States of America
10   9   8   7   6   5   4   3   2   1

Entry under main title:
Shadow Children: Understanding Education's #1 Problem

A RLD Publications book
Bibliography: p.
Includes index p. 183

ISBN: 0-9787610-0-6
Library of Congress Control Number: 2006931748

Dedicated to

The lost ones and their relentless retrievers

Table of Contents

SECTION III: The Syndrome of Shadow Children

SECTION IV: Prevention and Intervention: Where It Should All Begin . . .

Acknowledgements

INITIAL recognition goes to the children who made this book necessary: little battered bodies and crushed hearts, warped minds and twisted spirits, coming from their often poor substitute for a family into the schools to be fixed by teachers ill-equipped to do so.

Now, onto those caring teachers—and you know who you are! A wonderful and perhaps weary ARME (At-Risk Mindful Educators) of warriors stepping up to the plate and willing to try hard, make mistakes, and persevere, but never, ever quitting because they know that the longer one keeps swinging, the more young lives will be saved. They don't know which students are going to be saved, but it doesn't matter because they know some *will be*, and that's all real champions need to know.

Every preteacher went to college thinking they were going to teach science, elementary school, history, English, math, kindergarten, or physical education, but some found their hearts surprisingly pulled in the direction of teaching at-risk children instead. Out of necessity and without preparation, they donned the hats of the social worker, the nurse, the counselor, the friend, and sometimes the parent and provider and attempted to impart what knowledge they could when they could. They placed the kids' needs *first*, ahead of curriculum guides! This is what makes them the champions for children that they are. There is a conspiracy to protect parents and positions more than the children in many school systems, and *these brave teachers will have none of it*!

To these angel-warrior teachers: Stand tall—tall enough to see each other above the average certified crowd—and reach out to share best practices with one another, and deliberately stay in frequent contact giving the hope and strength necessary never to surrender in this fight against the growing tragedy of our sacrificial children.

More than likely, you are the last chance they have.

Remember, at the time, not all at-risk kids appreciated what their great teachers did for them. So this is to *you*, former at-risk kids: Buy thank you cards, and make a point to write those teachers and tell them how you were helped. They need to hear it from you more than anyone. Down deep you know what they did for you was worth much more than a card, so donate a few minutes to thanking them. It's all they really want.

Thank You to the National At-Risk Education Network staff for their ongoing work and support:

Amy—Assistant Director
Mark—Systems Analyst and Data Assistance
TJ—IT and Hardware Professional
Ron—Webmaster
Zak—Graphic Design

The National At-Risk Education Network Board and Advisory Council, plus all of our associates and subscribers

Marian College:
Dr. David Boers, Professor of At-Risk Education
Dr. Carleen VandeZande, Professor of Curriculum Development

Introduction

I grabbed Bob's muscular arm before he could slam his fist angrily onto the table again. The judge looked at us, a scowl starting to cross his face, replacing the deadpan look that had been there, but I couldn't shut Bob's mouth.

"That's lame!" he exclaimed, his face reddening, "That is so damn lame!"

Suddenly, I had visions of calling my wife from jail, "Honey, I can't dine with your parents tonight because I am having collards and corn bread with the fellas in the jail cafeteria."

Even the hardened social worker, who had probably dealt with most every sordid form of abuse that the rest of us don't even want to know about, jumped.

Bob was undaunted, "Judge, you just *can not* send Lydia back into that home, for Chrissakes!"

Lucky for Bob, lucky for me, Judge Wilson was a juvenile judge. Lucky for both of us, we were in chambers and not in his court where he would have had little choice but to slap us with contempt charges.

"Calm down, Bob." Judge Seymour's face softened, "I appreciate what you're attempting, but there's really not much that I can do."

Ann Bennett, the Tallahassee social worker, relaxed a little and straightened her attractive red skirt, while I took a deep breath.

Bob was not finished. "Well, this just bites! This kid comes into my class the day after Christmas vacation with scabs on her back the size of leeches after her drunken dad—if you can call him that—beats her half to death for a Merry Christmas morning, and you're going to put her back in there! Holy crap!"

The judge's scowl was back. Ann stiffened again. I could smell the fatback cooking. I grabbed Bob's arm yet again.

"Please understand, Judge," I quickly interceded. "This little girl was beaten, not only for something she didn't do, but then she received no medical attention and had to sleep on a mattress on the floor with eight younger brothers and sisters for the next eight days until she came back to school and the nurse could treat her."

I was quite naïve. It was 1969 and I was 28 years old, doing my administrative internship in an elementary school as part of my graduate studies at Florida State University. Bob and I had become friends because he was a champion for have-nothing kids. He personally stocked a little store in the supply room off his sixth-grade classroom. He had combs, toothbrushes, toothpaste, healthy snacks, clothes, soap, barrettes, and all kinds of little goodies for 11 year olds. He had an arrangement with the nurse to take certain at-risk kids down to the shower in her office and get them all cleaned up for the day. If the kids took their showers, brushed their teeth, and combed their hair, they could pick something out of his store. He was always making home visits, checking up on "his kids," buying things for them with his own money, doing for them whatever they needed in order to have a decent sixth-grade year. His classroom was a whirlwind of activity centers, filled with laughter and high-energy learning. Bob had designed and implemented a program that established Youth Tutoring Youth (YTY), the first program in Leon County whereby unmotivated, unsuccessful sixth-grade readers spent an hour a day teaching first graders beginning reading and how to make picture dictionaries. He was always doing things like that.

Lydia was a major project of Bob's. Her mother picked up sticks for a living. She and a group of Black women moved quickly ahead of the tung nut harvesting machines picking up sticks so that they didn't gum up the tines. If they moved too slowly, they were whipped by white foremen with bigger sticks. She had done this for 20 years and was permanently stooped over as a result.

Lydia's biological father worked in a mill during the day and drank every night. He loved to beat people, especially helpless people like his wife and his children. The times I talked to him I was sure he was brain damaged. The daughter, Lydia, was becoming damaged in her own way. Bob was trying to rescue her. She came to school filthy and had (we discovered later) most every intestinal parasite known, including Ascaris, tape worm, and some little tiny nocturnal parasites that make your anus itch all night long as they crawl in and out to lay eggs.

A visit by Ann to Lydia's home, on Bob's recommendation after his first visit, revealed that they had no running water, a broken refrigerator, and a propane stove that wouldn't work anymore (explaining the pile of rotting boxes of unused federal beans and rice on the front porch). Ann reported that there also was no toilet, and the family just relieved themselves in the woods over a log—uphill of their well.

Bob had worked hard to get Lydia lice-free, to begin taking pride in her showering, teeth brushing, and hair combing each school morning down in Nurse Green's clinic. She was really making progress and had begun, after three months, to start smiling. At the Christmas party on the last day of school, Bob gave Lydia a dozen oranges to take home to her family for the holidays. When she got home, her mother put them up on a rafter to be saved for Christmas Day. The next day, Lydia was to babysit all of her brothers and sisters while her parents went off to work. Over her frantic protests, four of Lydia's brothers took down the oranges and ate them, sharing them with the little kids. Lydia refused to eat any and knew there would be hell to pay. The boys probably did, too, but hunger quickly drives out reason.

When the father came home drunk on Christmas morning and was told by the mother what had happened, the father grabbed a piece of fan belt, took Lydia into the front yard, and beat her across the back until she fainted. She was then sent to bed with no supper and received nothing to eat for several days. Eight days later when she came back to school, the nurse saw the scabs—many over four inches long and a half inch wide on her back—and called the authorities.

The parents were in the courtroom, nervously waiting to see what the White judge was going to do to the poor Black folks. The judge had taken one look at the papers, the charges, and the pathetic sniveling parents and had called Bob, myself, and the school social worker into his chambers.

Judge Wilson looked at Bob, "Don't think I am not going to put the fear of God into them, Bob. I am going to scare the hell out of them, but . . ."

Bob stared back, "But what?"

I cringed, definitely feeling Bob was pushing it to the breaking point. Secretly, I admired his willingness to risk arguing with a judge, but it was probably useless, and this became apparent as the judge continued.

"Bob," he nodded at us, "Tony, Ann. Face it. First of all, the foster homes in Tallahassee are full. And secondly," he lowered his voice, "who is going to take in a poor Black sixth grader in this town?"

It went down hill from there as was indicated by the rest of the hearing. The judge threatened the parents. The mother cried repeatedly, "Don't take my baby from me!" And the Dad just hung and shook his scarred, shaved head and acted repentant for what he couldn't even remember doing.

Lydia went home with her parents.

Similar stories like this are repeated in America many times daily. And these are only the abused and neglected children that come to light. *How many stay in the shadows?* It is tragic how many. But *it's real!*

Every day in America[1]:

- 4 children are killed by abuse or neglect.
- 1 young person dies from HIV infection.
- 5 children commit suicide.
- 8 children are killed by firearms.
- 181 children are arrested for violent crimes.
- 1,154 babies are born to teen mothers.
- 2,482 children are confirmed as abused or neglected
- 2,447 babies are born into poverty.
- 2,756 children drop out of high school every school day (1 of every 4 high school freshmen fails to finish high school in the United States of America).
- 4,356 children are arrested.

This is every day! Multiply these figures (except for the dropout numbers) by 365 for truly disturbing annual totals.

How can children enduring the suffering implied by these statistics succeed in school? Not very well, and certainly not if the school system is insensitive and nonsupportive and has no compensatory programs in place.

---

[1] Data source: Children's Defense Fund 2005 Annual Report—Washington, D.C.

In the United States:[2]

- 8,400,000 children are without health insurance.
- 13,027,000 children live in poverty.

How can children who have little or no health care, and/or who live in poverty succeed in school? Not very well and certainly not if the school system is insensitive and non-supportive and has no compensatory programs in place.

> We are in a war, and we must wake up, arm ourselves,
> and unite in the effort to save the young people of our country.

[2]Data source: U.S. Census Bureau Current Population Survey, 2004.

CHAPTER 1

Who Are Shadow Children?

O NE of the goals of this book is to make the invisible visible, to bring into awareness that of which we were previously unaware, to bring into the foreground what was formerly background, to bring into the light what was once in the shadows. These are the at-risk children. They are often easy to miss despite the fact that they desperately need to be seen and serviced. The cost of continuing to ignore this problem will stagger you.

In later chapters I will detail many of the facets of the Shadow Children issue. But, first, let me begin to make the invisible visible clearly.

First, why bother coming up with yet another new category of kids with issues? Unlike *Indigo Children*, which Lee Carroll and Jan Tober claim are born that way, Shadow Children are created. They are products of their environment. What I mean by the *environment* is represented mostly by the authoritative people around them that shape them. Usually, it is that entity we call *the parents*. Children, although genetically determined in some ways (hair color, eye color, etc.), are quite malleable in other ways left open by the genetic map during the early years and shaped by the type of parenting practices, or lack thereof.

There is serious debate over exactly what the term *at-risk* means. Some deny there is a need for such a term. We will examine this denial and the cover-ups that exist and why they happen.

As the director of the National At-Risk Education Network, I am admittedly biased toward its two-pronged definition for the term *at-risk youth*:

1. At-risk of dropping out of school
2. At-risk of not succeeding in life because of being raised in unfavorable circumstances

Sometimes a student falls into both categories, but all Shadow Children fall into at least one. Schools need to be ready to support them in either or both.

How Can the Tide Be Turned?

When you are a Shadow Child, you feel the price tag every day. You feel it as a deficit in various parts of your being: your emotions, your finances, your health, your relationships, your spirit, your limited opportunities, your thought processes—any or all of these. You don't need any convincing that the weight of being a Shadow Child is too heavy. As an adult, if you are still toting your baggage, you will usually not be able to better your lot in life until you come to realize:

I may not be responsible for what happened to me as a child,
but I am 100% responsible for my own recovery.

Individually, the efforts and costs of recovery are unique and not always external. They may involve quantities in life such as money and possessions but, more often, for the survivor the personal issues are about qualities of life: meaningfulness, fulfillment, vitality, and that mysterious thing called happiness. Each Shadow Child has a story worthy of study, and each Shadow Child is worth the effort it takes for remediation; however, to intervene on a larger community, state, or even national scale will take a different kind of awareness. To remedy in our society the mechanisms that (1) create a Shadow Child population and (2) fail to rehabilitate the Shadow Child population once created, we need to create campaigns of various sorts. There are three equally valid approaches to directly impact people with those campaigns.

The first valid approach is appealing to a sense of *injustice*: These poor children! It's not fair! No kid asked to be placed at risk! If you have been a Shadow Child, this approach usually reaches you. You know what it is like to be kicked while down or to have no one mentoring you who is healthy and there for you when you need them, or to be shunned, shamed, abused, or neglected or to live a life of restriction in poverty.

Oprah Winfrey comes to mind. She has admitted her childhood anguish on public television, and you can tell that she feels for the downtrodden because of it. Her role in *The Color Purple* is a tribute to her feelings about encouraging others to use their anger to rise above the abuse and live a good life. Campaigns touting the injustices befalling Shadow Children will reach certain segments of the population who have been there and move them to action.

The second valid campaign approach is via *compassion*. If you are a person of unusual compassion, you have a tender heart, the ability to empathize, and a willingness to believe and respect others' experiences without having to experience them yourself. Princess Diana and her work with children with AIDS comes to mind. Has there ever been a more impassioned speech than hers at an AIDS Conference in Edinburgh in September of 1993? In part, she stated:

> And what of the children who live with HIV every day? Not because they're necessarily ill themselves, but because their family life includes a mother, father, brother or sister who has the virus. How will we help them come to terms with the loss of the people they love? How will we help them to grieve? How will we help them to feel secure about their future?

> These children need to feel the same things as other children. To play, to laugh and cry, to make friends, to enjoy the ordinary experiences of childhood. To feel loved and nurtured and included by the world they live in, without the stigma that AIDS continues to attract. By listening to their needs, really listening, perhaps we can find the best way of helping these children to face their future with greater confidence and hope.

Princess Diana never had AIDS. How could she tap into those issues so well? Compassion, insight, openness to others' experiences, and humanitarian concern seemed to emanate from her. Compassionate campaigns will reach certain population segments enough to move them to proactive contributions of energy and resources to help bring about a remedy.

The third valid approach is through reason. The best vehicle for this approach is often looking at the efficiency and money issues of the problem(s) created by having a population of Shadow Children.

What Is the Cost of Having a Population of Shadow Children?

Few people realize the financial aspects of having a population of

Shadow Children (who grow into adults and often raise more Shadow Children), and the reader may be quite unpleasantly surprised at the gigantic price tag for not doing something about this crisis—not just on a human level, but also on an economic level. Hopefully, the following data will be used to leverage (justify) more realistic expenditures for prevention and intervention programs in the future because basically the message is going to be: *You can pay now, or pay a whole lot more later.*

The Cost of Child Abuse and Neglect

We shall look at several cost factors in the Shadow Child arena in the next chapter. There is no place better to start than with the incredible cost of child abuse and neglect. Almost every Shadow Child is that way because of child abuse and neglect in some form. Child abuse and neglect cost our society dearly, not only in terms of the trauma caused to the maltreated individuals, but also in economic terms. Economic costs include the funds spent each year on child welfare services for abused and neglected children, as well as the large sums dedicated to addressing the short- and long-term consequences of abuse and neglect. Effective prevention programs that promote the safety and well-being of children and families hold potential for lessening the suffering and trauma experienced by children and for greatly reducing these economic costs.

To date, few in-depth and rigorous financial analyses have been conducted to give us a solid understanding of the total costs of maltreatment (i.e., the costs of *not* preventing child abuse and neglect), as compared to the economic savings associated with prevention. Nevertheless, several prevention advocates, researchers, and evaluators have begun to grapple with these issues. We begin with a discussion of the cost elements that make up the total cost of child maltreatment. The second chapter highlights findings from selected studies that have conducted cost-benefit and cost-of-failure analyses.

CHAPTER 2

Child Maltreatment Costs[3,4]

CHILD abuse and neglect have caused detrimental effects on the physical, psychological, cognitive, and behavioral development of children (National Research Council, 1993). These consequences range from minor to severe and include physical injuries, brain damage, chronic low self-esteem, problems with bonding and forming relationships, developmental delays, learning disorders, and aggressive behavior. Clinical conditions associated with abuse and neglect include depression, post-traumatic stress disorder, and conduct disorders. Beyond the trauma inflicted on individual children, child maltreatment also has been linked with long-term, negative societal consequences. For example, studies associate child maltreatment with increased risk of low academic achievement, drug use, teen pregnancy, juvenile delinquency, and adult criminality (Widom, 1992; Kelley, Thornberry, and Smith, 1997). Further, these consequences cost society by expanding the need for mental health and substance abuse treatment programs, police and court interventions, correctional facilities, and public assistance programs and by causing losses in productivity. Calculation of the total financial cost of child maltreatment must

---

[3]Information for much of this section on costing is provided with excerption permission from the National Clearinghouse on Child Abuse and Neglect (NCCAN).

[4]Another great authoritative source of well-documented figures is *Saving Lives, Saving Dollars: Mitigating the Impact of Child Maltreatment*, January 2006, by Bruce Jacobs, Ph.D. (ed.), Department of Extension Home Economics, College of Agriculture and Home Economics, New Mexico State University, Las Cruces, NM.

account for both the direct costs and the indirect costs of its long-term consequences.

Direct Costs

Direct costs reflect expenditures incurred by the child welfare system as well as the judicial, law enforcement, health care, and mental health systems in responding to abused and neglected children and their families. Direct costs include expenses associated with hospitalization and medical services provided to treat injuries resulting from abuse, child protective services (CPS) and/or police investigations; foster care and other out-of-home placement services for maltreated children; and family preservation, rehabilitation, and treatment programs.

Government expenditures for child welfare programs provide a benchmark for estimating a portion of the annual direct costs of child abuse and neglect. For fiscal year 1998, federal expenditures to states for major child welfare programs exceeded $4.5 billion. This figure includes child welfare services, foster care, adoption assistance, and family preservation and support but excludes Medicaid dollars, an important source of treatment funding for children and families. Based on a survey of state child welfare agencies (CWLA, 1997), federal funding accounts for less than half (42%) of state child welfare expenditures, with the remainder supported by state (49%) and local (9%) funding.

A study by the Missouri Children's Trust Fund (1997) provides a different lens through which to view direct costs of maltreatment. The study analyzed the direct economic costs of one type of child maltreatment, shaken baby syndrome (SBS), in Missouri over a 10-year period. The study found that the state spent at least $6.9 million, or approximately $32,500 on each of the 214 identified SBS victims. These costs included $4 million in Medicaid expenses, $1.9 million for Division of Family Services expenditures, and nearly $1 million for Department of Mental Health services.

Indirect Costs

Indirect costs reflect the long-term economic consequences of child maltreatment in such areas as special education, mental health, substance abuse, teen pregnancy, welfare dependency, domestic violence, homelessness, juvenile delinquency, and adult criminality.

Indirect costs are more difficult to assess than direct costs, and frequently, calculations are based on assumptions, or they are extrapolated from research. For example, Deborah Daro (1988) estimated a national indirect juvenile delinquency cost of $14.9 million based on the following: an estimated 177,300 adolescent maltreatment victims nationwide in 1983; research indicating a 20 percent delinquency rate among adolescent victims; and average costs ($21,000 per year) for 2 years of correctional institutionalization for these abused and delinquent youth. The same analysis estimated that, if 1 percent of severely abused children were to suffer permanent disabilities, the annual cost of community services for treating children with developmental disabilities would increase by $1.1 million.

Indirect costs also may include inferred costs of lost productivity associated with injury, incarceration, long-term unemployment, or death. For example, Daro's (1988) cost analysis projected that the national cost in future lost productivity of severely abused or neglected children is between $658 million and $1.3 billion each year, assuming that their impairments reduce their future earnings by as little as 5–10 percent. A Michigan study (Caldwell, 1992) used rates of per capita income and average lifetime participation in the labor force to generate average lifetime earnings of, and calculate lost tax revenue from, those children who died as a result of child abuse or preventable infant mortality. The study concluded that, in addition to the devastating personal losses experienced by the families of the infants and children who died, the state lost an estimated $46 million in tax revenue. (Although this figure represents the loss of tax revenue over a lifetime, it can also be interpreted as the per year loss to the state if the rates of tax, abuse, and mortality remain relatively stable.)

As the above examples show, the total financial costs of child abuse and neglect can be quite high. Conversely, the potential benefits or savings from prevention also are high. These costs and potential savings form the basis of cost-benefit analyses.

Prevention Cost-Benefit Analyses

Few in-depth economic analyses have been conducted to assess the cost-effectiveness of child abuse prevention. Four key studies, presented below, compare the costs of preventive family support services with the savings generated from the positive outcomes of prevention programs and/or the direct and indirect costs of not preventing child maltreatment. Many prevention programs, including those referenced in the studies below, address not only prevention of child abuse and neglect, but also prevention of other threats to child and family well-being. Examples of such threats include preventable health conditions (e.g., low birth weight, infant mortality, newborn addictions), lack of economic self-sufficiency, social isolation, lack of parenting skills or knowledge, and inappropriate child-rearing behaviors. Several of these other threats also represent precursors or risk factors associated with abuse and neglect. As such, the benefits generated by addressing these risk factors are included in this broad view of the costs related to child maltreatment.

Case Studies

NCCAN provides four case studies to illustrate how costing is computed in various scenarios. These are included to give the reader some insight into the reasoning behind the twists and turns of gathering accurate data in a complex and convoluted financial situation.

Elmira, New York

A report by David Olds and colleagues (1993) presents an economic analysis within a rigorous evaluation based on a randomized trial of a nurse home visitation program serving 400 pregnant women in Elmira, New York. The evaluation indicated that frequent home visits by nurses during pregnancy and the first 2 years of the child's life improved a wide range of maternal and child health outcomes among adolescent, unmarried, and low-income, first-time mothers (Olds & Kitzman, 1993). The study found that, in contrast to women assigned to the comparison group, nurse-visited women experienced: (1) improved health-related behaviors (e.g., reduced cigarette use and improved diets) and use of prenatal services during pregnancy, (2) fewer emergency room visits for children during the second year of life, (3) greater workforce participation; and (4) fewer subsequent pregnancies for low-income and unmarried women. In addition, among poor, unmarried teenage women, the study observed a 75 percent reduction in state-verified cases of child abuse and neglect during the first 2 years of a child's life.

The economic analysis for the Elmira home visitation program concluded that government savings could offset the program costs for low-income participants within 4 years (Olds et al., 1993). The analysis estimated an average cost of $3,133 per family (1980 dollars) for providing home visitation services to low-income participants, based on expenditures for nurses' salaries, benefits, supplies, and transportation. These costs were compared with reduced expenditures in other government programs affected by the positive outcomes of home visitation. The economic impact of improved maternal and child functioning was evaluated from a standpoint of four government programs—Aid to Families with Dependent Children (AFDC), Medicaid, Food Stamps, and Child Protective Services (CPS)—as well as increased tax revenues generated by subsequent employment. Within low-income families, for the 4-year period following the child's birth, the estimated per family government savings was $3,498 (Olds et al., 1993). The majority of estimated government savings (based on comparison group expenditures) was derived from reductions in AFDC and food stamp payments, which were associated with increased employment and reduced subsequent pregnancies among program clients.

Michigan

A 1992 study for the Michigan Children's Trust Fund (Caldwell, 1992) concluded that providing either comprehensive parent education or home visitation service for every Michigan family expecting its first child would amount to only 5 percent of the estimated total state cost of maltreatment. Based on an estimated per-family cost of $712, statewide prevention services were projected at approximately $43 million. In comparison, analysts figured that child maltreatment and inadequate prenatal care cost the state approximately $823 million. Michigan's total estimated annual cost of child maltreatment and inadequate prenatal care included direct and indirect costs associated with the following:

- protective services ($38 million)
- foster care ($74 million)
- health costs of low birth weight babies ($256 million)
- medical treatment of injuries caused by abuse ($5 million)

- special education costs ($6 million)
- psychological care for child maltreatment victims ($16 million)
- juvenile justice system and correction services ($207 million)
- adult criminality ($175 million)
- projected tax revenue lost from infant deaths ($46 million).

In making these estimates, a series of extrapolations were used to account for the proportion of total spending that can be linked to maltreatment. For example, prior research (Loeber & Stouthamer-Loeber, 1987) suggests that approximately 20 percent of children from abusive homes commit delinquent acts as juveniles and 25 percent of these go on to commit crimes as adults. Based on these findings, the Michigan researchers predicted that, of the 39,452 children identified as abused that year, 1,996 would become involved in the adult criminal justice system. With an average annual state adult prison cost of $25,000 and an average prison sentence of 3.5 years, total adult criminality associated with child abuse and neglect was estimated to cost $175 million (1,996 × $25,000 × 3.5).

Colorado

A similar 1995 analysis, commissioned by the Colorado Children's Trust Fund, examined the costs incurred in the state of Colorado by failing to prevent child abuse and neglect and then compared these costs with the savings that would accrue from an investment in effective prevention services (Gould & O'Brien, 1995). The state estimated $190 million in annual direct costs for child maltreatment, including the costs of CPS investigations, child welfare services to children in their own homes, and out-of-home placements. In addition, annual indirect costs were calculated based on an assumption that $212 million (approximately 20 percent of the $1 billion total expenditure) in state social programs were associated with the long-term consequences to individuals maltreated as children (e.g., special education, AFDC assistance payments, job training programs, youth institutional and community programs, mental health programs for children and adults, substance and drug abuse programs, victim services, criminal justice programs, domestic violence shelters, and prisons). Indirect costs ($212 million) and direct costs ($190 million) combined for an estimated total of $402 million in annual expenditures related to abuse and neglect.

The state costs of maltreatment were compared to the potential savings associated with an intensive home visitor prevention program targeted toward those families most at risk of abuse and neglect. Based on an estimated $2,000 per-family cost of a statewide home visitation program for high-risk families with children from birth to 3 years old, the Colorado analysis projected total costs of $32 million. At the time of the study, $8 million was being spent in the state on home visitation and family support, thus suggesting a need for $24 million in new money. The Colorado analysis concluded that, if the program were able to reduce child maltreatment expenditure by only 6 percent (.06 × $402 million annual expenditure), the cost of the prevention investment would be offset.

Allegheny County, Pennsylvania

In a recent study, Bruner (1996) used statistical modeling to estimate benefits or savings as the potential returns on investment from family centers for high-risk neighborhoods in Allegheny County, Pennsylvania. This study approaches the cost of failure by contrasting the level of spending on remediation, maintenance, and CPS for residents living in the highest risk, distressed neighborhoods of the county with the level of spending in lower risk neighborhoods in the same county. This approach captures real-world comparisons for estimates of "what could be" (Bruner, 1996).

The study first determined the potential savings obtainable by transforming the high-risk neighborhoods into neighborhoods similar to the rest of Allegheny County. This potential savings, or cost of failure, included expenditures across a number of public spending areas most associated with preventable maltreatment and health problems in childhood AFDC and Medicaid, food stamps, children and youth social services, juvenile justice, jail and prison, and lost economic activity and tax revenue. The analysis concluded that the county would save approximately $565 million annually in public spending, or $416.3 million, if these costs were discounted over a 20-year timeframe.

Costs were calculated for establishing family centers to serve populations within the high-risk neighborhoods. This analysis was grounded in the existing body of research on the various elements needed for children to succeed, the principles of effective frontline practice, and the potential long-term effects of such strategies upon child outcomes. The study projected that to serve 45–60 percent of all families with very young children in Allegheny County high-risk neighborhoods would require an expansion of funding of $11.9 million, from $6.6 million (for existing centers with a capacity for 2,640 families) to $18.5 million (to serve up to 8,400 families).

From a return-on-investment perspective, the $18.5 million expenditure can be compared with the $416.3 million estimated long-term preventable expenditures. An $18.5 million investment would have to contribute to reducing such preventable financial costs by only 5 percent for it to be considered cost-effective.

Conclusion

In each of the above studies, the analysts concluded that the positive outcomes of prevention programs, with even relatively small reductions in the rate of child maltreatment, demonstrate that prevention can be cost-effective. Although much remains to be learned about the optimal levels of investment in prevention, these studies present a starting point for continued analysis and discussion.

To estimate the financial costs of the long-term consequences of child maltreatment on adolescent and adult development and behavior, cost-benefit analyses must take a holistic and long-term perspective. Most of the investments in prevention, particularly as they apply to investments in families with young children, are likely to have "payback curves" that extend over a long period of time, with much of the savings occurring when the child reaches a healthy, productive, and nonviolent adulthood (Bruner and Scott, 1994). While additional investment, research, careful documentation, and well-designed analysis is needed within the prevention field—both to assess the effectiveness of prevention programs its cost-effectiveness—current findings suggest that, over the long term, *prevention pays*.

Funded by a grant from the Edna McConnell Clark Foundation in 2001, Prevent Child Abuse America conducted a study using conservative estimates, meaning those standards set down by the U.S.

Department of Health and Human Services harm standard, the most stringent classification category. In addition, they did not attempt to quantify all the indirect costs of abuse and neglect including the provision of welfare benefits to adults whose economic condition is a direct result of abuse and neglect. Even with this conservative estimating the figure came out to *$94,000,000,000* a year!

This is how they computed it:

DIRECT COSTS

Statistical Justification Data

Hospitalization

Rationale: 565,000 children were reported as suffering serious harm from abuse in 1993. One of the less severe injuries is a broken or fractured bone. Cost of treating a fracture or dislocation of the radius or ulna per incident is $10,983.

Calculation: 565,000 × $10,983

$6,205,395,000

Chronic Health Problems

Rationale: 30 percent of maltreated children suffer chronic medical problems. The cost of treating a child with asthma per incident in the hospital is $6,410.

Calculations: .30 × 1,553,800 = 446,140; 446,140 × $6,410

$2,987,957,400

Mental Health Care System

Rationale: 743,200 children were abused in 1993. For purposes of obtaining a conservative estimate, neglected children are not included. One of the costs to the mental health care system is counseling. Estimated cost per family for counseling is $2,860. One in five abused children is estimated to receive these services.

Calculations: 743,200/5 = 148,640; 148,640 × $2,860

$425,110,400

Child Welfare System

Rationale: The Urban Institute published a paper in 1999 reporting on the results of a study it conducted estimating child welfare costs associated with child abuse and neglect to be $14.4 billion.

$14,400,000,000

Law Enforcement

Rationale: The National Institute of Justice estimates the following costs of police services for each of the following interventions: child sexual abuse ($56); physical abuse ($20); emotional abuse ($20) and child educational neglect ($2). Cross-referenced against DHHS statistics on number of each incidents occurring annually.

Calculations: Physical Abuse—381,700 × $20 = $7,634,000; Sexual Abuse—217,700 × $56 = $12,191,200; Emotional Abuse—204,500 × $20 = $4,090,000; and Educational Neglect—397,300 × $2 = $794,600

$24,709,800

Judicial System

Rationale: The Dallas Commission on Children and Youth determined the cost per initiated court action for each case of child maltreatment was $1,372.34.

Approximately 16 percent of child abuse victims have court action taken on their behalf. Calculations: 1,553,800 cases nationwide × .16 = 248,608 victims with court action; 248,608 × $1,372.34

$341,174,702

Total Direct Costs $24,384,347,302

INDIRECT COSTS

Statistical Justification Data

Special Education

Rationale: More than 22 percent of abused children have a learning disorder requiring special education. Total cost per child for learning disorders is $655 per year.

Calculations: 1,553,800 × .22 = 341,386; 341,386 × $655

$223,607,830

Mental Health and Health Care

The health care cost per woman related to child abuse and neglect is $8,175,816/163,844=$50. If the costs were similar for men, we could estimate that $50 × 185,105,441 adults in the United States cost the nation $9,255,272,050. However, the costs for men are likely to be very different, and a more conservative estimate would be half of that amount.

$4,627,636,025

Juvenile Delinquency

Rationale: 26 percent of children who are abused or neglected become delinquents, compared to 17 percent of children as a whole, for a difference of 9 percent. Cost per year per child for incarceration is $62,966. Average length of incarceration in Michigan is 15 months.

Calculations: $0.09 \times 1,553,800 = 139,842$; $139,842 \times \$62,966 = \$8,805,291,372$

$8,805,291,372

Lost Productivity to Society

Rationale: Abused and neglected children grow up to be disproportionately affected by unemployment and underemployment. Lost productivity has been estimated at $656 million to $1.3 billion. Conservative estimate is used.

$656,000,000

Adult Criminality

Rationale: Violent crime in U.S. costs $426 billion per year. According to the National Institute of Justice, 13 percent of all violence can be linked to earlier child maltreatment.

Calculations: $\$426$ billion $\times .13$

$55,380,000,000

Total Indirect Costs $69,692,535,227

GRAND TOTAL COST $94,076,882,529 Annually!

Other costs should be included because at-risk kids often grow up with illiteracy, drug and alcohol issues, mental health issues, and wind-up-in-jail issues. Look at the following facts:

- Drug abuse costs society $97,000,000,000 annually (National Clearinghouse for Alcohol and Drug Information).
- Alcohol abuse costs society $148,000,000,000 annually (National Clearinghouse for Alcohol and Drug Information).
- One full year of imprisonment costs approximately $18,400 per person (National Institute on Drug Abuse), and there are just over 2,222,331 people in federal, state, and local prisons (U.S. Department of Justice) annually costing us a grand total of $40,000,000,000 for jailing people in this country.

Although we have no annual cost figures for the following, one knows there has to be a high price tag attached to the following statistics:

- 1,700,000 teen runaways (National Center for Missing and Exploited Children)
- child depression—1 in 33 children and 1 in 8 adolescents (National Mental Health Association)
- 1,800 youths commit suicide yearly
- 3,000,000 teens annually acquire a sexually transmitted disease (STD) (American Social Health Association)
- health issues raised by the 4,000,000 teen smokers who will join the ranks of 45,000,000 adult smokers (Center for Disease Control)

But we do know, according to the Center for Disease Control, that 90 percent of smoking, alcoholism, inappropriate drug use, depression, and unhealthy sexual habits start in youth. In other words, these financial concerns are more than likely seeded in the world of the Shadow Children.

The total price tag is almost too large to comprehend because it is approaching, if not exceeding, $400,000,000,000 *annually*. But what is not too large for comprehension is that we have an abundance of financial data that justifies a substantial increase in prevention and intervention funding for Shadow Children. Of that, there can be little doubt. If your child is or was one of the previous statistics, you probably needed little convincing.

Section I

Shadow Children:
Type I—The School Dropout

CHAPTER 3

Youth at Risk of Dropping Out of School

FACTS we know: According to the 2004 figures from the Children's Defense Fund, one of every eight school children will not graduate. The U.S. census school enrollment projections for the year 2004 were 54,400,000 children. This means that the population currently at risk of dropping out could be as many as 6,800,000 children. However, the U.S. Department of Education states that 30 percent of America's youth will not receive a high school diploma. That comes to 16,033,500 children. How we could have this almost 10,000,000 child discrepancy is covered in Chapters 6 and 7.

The financial future of high school dropouts is grim. Figures illustrating significant differences in potential monetary success, some surprising, are included below.

Why Is Dropping Out Such a Poor Choice?

One must never underestimate the social stigma of dropping out. Unless they are successful, make it big (and very few do), no adult sincerely and seriously brags about having quit school. They are ashamed. They know society looks down on the dropout. Along with this, not always, but often, come the accompanying illiteracy and narrow knowledge base of the young person that drops out.

Tragic, also, is the series of events that precede the actual moment of dropping out of school. Leading up to the moment of the act of dropping out, there had to be so many quality of life issues such as boredom, confusion, fear, and angst on a daily basis. All these painful experiences are then topped off by a loss of respect for and appreciation of what the phrase *good education* means and the feeling that school is not only a terrible place, but academic learning is a painful experience.

These experiences are fairly personalized issues and depend on the students and their values and attitudes and the situational specifics. What is standard across the population, however, is the issue of loss of income and what that brings. There are many official statistics that make this issue quite clear.

The Dollar Cost of Dropping Out of School

First, let's discuss mean annual earning by age and the highest level of school completed. These figures are based solely on year-round, full-time workers aged 18 and over who were in the civilian labor force, worked, and had earnings in 2000.

Total Education	Average Annual Income for Life
Less than 9th-grade education	$20,998
9th–12th grade, no diploma	$21,490
High school graduate	$32,020
Some college (including Associate degrees)	$39,125
Bachelor's degree	$63,216
Master's degree	$76,340
Terminal or professional degree	$100,230

If you believe that money enables one to have better health and prosperity, including all the emotional aspects from security to self-actualization, then the picture is pretty stark for not staying in school.

There is also quite an incentive for advancing one's education. To state it quite plainly:

- Some high school is worth $1,000 additional income per year.
- A high school diploma is worth $10,000 more per year.
- Some college is worth almost another $7,100 per year.
- A college degree is worth a whopping $24,000 more per year.

- A master's degree is worth an additional $13,000.
- And a terminal graduate or professional degree is worth another $24,000 per year.

Note: This means the difference between income for a dropout and a graduate degree is almost $78,000 per year for every income earning year—almost $3,500,000 on the average per lifetime.

Multiply any of the above amounts by the average number of working years in any person's life. Is this a big enough reason to do whatever it takes to keep kids in school? Think about the children they will raise when they have a family and what kind of influence that differential will make in their readiness, health, and socialization skills!

There are still bigger implications in these figures. The figures you have been viewing were for men only. Let us do the same figures for women.

Again, these figures are based on year-round, full-time, female workers aged 18 and over who were in the civilian labor force and had earnings in 2000.

Total Education	Average Annual Income for Life
Less than 9th-grade education	$12,665
9th–12th grade, no diploma	$12,698
High school graduate	$19,269
Some college (including Associate degrees)	$23,433
Bachelor's degree	$35,083
Master's degree	$45,517
Terminal or professional degree	$58,016

Now let us place the two charts side by side:

Total Education	Men	Women
Less than 9th-grade education	$20,998	$12,665
9th–12th grade, no diploma	$21,940	$12,698
High school graduate	$32,020	$19,269
Some college (including Associate degrees)	$39,125	$23,433
Bachelor's degree	$63,216	$35,083
Master's degree	$76,340	$45,517
Terminal or professional degree	$100,230	$58,016

Remember, this is the annual average income and must be multiplied by every year of one's life to get the full impact. The disparity is so large that it makes for a depressing message.

Start looking at female students differently. What do they need from their time in school to truly take their position as economic equals in tomorrow's world?

Implications

Explaining the gender disparity in salaries per grade level achieved could spawn much speculation and discussion, but regardless of conclusions drawn, one can draw a clear implication from the following statistic: each and every year in the United States, approximately 821,980 babies are born to unmarried mothers who did not complete high school.[5] The predictably limited resources that will be available to these mothers and their children speak volumes about being at risk of many things.

[5]Children's Defense Fund 2005 Annual Report, Washington, D.C.

CHAPTER 4

Danger in the Shadows

VISITED a school during session lately? Busy, busy, and busy—a lot going on in a constant buzz of activity. I certainly do not have what it takes anymore to do what today's teachers do. Sometimes I think what has evolved slowly over the centuries into the standard operating procedures of schools today is sheer madness. We think of it as normal only because it is prevalent and we have all been through it and have been acclimated. Think about it: A surrogate parent (teacher) sequestered all day with 25–35 foster kids in hard chairs under fluorescent lights in a room with a few square feet allocated per child. Each child comes to school, not empty, but with a full and diverse menu of personal, social, familial, emotional, and psychological needs ready to project onto the day (and each other). Add to this that subject matter is the last thing they want to focus on each of the 180 days when they come to school.

We say to the teacher, "Be a professional, forget your personal issues, get past each kid's personal agenda, and make sure No Child Is Left Behind academically." After all the passing out of workbooks and papers, recesses and lunch, fire drills, handing in stuff, student zoning out time, sharpening pencils, announcements, and maintenance interruptions, you have maybe three attentive hours a day for subject matter contact time, if you are lucky. You will be held accountable, and there will be consequences if your children do not progress 9 months' worth in 8 months.

And how, in the midst of this maelstrom, are you supposed to spot Cliff Evans?

Cipher in the Snow[6]

It started with tragedy on a biting cold February morning. I was driving behind the Milford Corners bus as I did most snowy mornings on my way to school. It veered and stopped short at the hotel, which it had no business doing, and I was annoyed as I had to come to an unexpected stop. A boy lurched out of the bus, reeled, stumbled, and collapsed on the snow bank at the curb. The bus driver and I reached him at the same moment. His thin, hollow face was white even against the snow.

"He's dead," the driver whispered.

It didn't register for a minute; I glanced quickly at the scared young faces staring down at us from the school bus. "A doctor! Quick! I'll phone from the hotel. . . ."

"No use; I tell you, he's dead." The driver looked down at the boy's still form. "He never even said he felt bad," he muttered. "Just tapped me on the shoulder and said, real quiet, 'I'm sorry. I have to get off at the hotel.' That's all. Polite and apologizing like."

At school, the giggling, shuffling morning noise quieted as news went down the halls. I passed a huddle of girls. "Who was it? Who dropped dead on the way to school?" I heard one of them half-whisper.

"Don't know his name. Some kid from Milford Corners," was the reply.

It was like that in the faculty room and the principal's office. "I'd appreciate your going out to tell the parents," the principal told me. "They haven't a phone, and anyway, somebody from the school should go there in person. I'll cover your classes."

"Why me?" I asked. "Wouldn't it be better if you did it?"

"I didn't know the boy," the principal admitted levelly. "And in last year's sophomore personalities column, I noted that you were listed as his favorite teacher."

I drove through the snow and cold down the bad canyon road to the Evans's place and thought about the boy, Cliff Evans. His favorite teacher! I thought. He hasn't spoken two words to me in 2 years! I could see him in my mind's eye all right, sitting back there in the last seat in

[6]Based on a true story by Jean Mizer in 1964, adapted by Carol Lynn Pearson in 1973 as a script for an educational film by the same name, produced by Brigham Young University and distributed by Encyclopedia Britannica.

my afternoon literature class. He came in the room by himself and left by himself. "Cliff Evans," I muttered to myself, "a boy who never talked." I thought a minute. "A boy who never smiled. I never saw him smile once."

The big ranch kitchen was clean and warm. I blurted out my news somehow. Mrs. Evans reached blindly toward a chair. "He never said anything about bein' ailing."

His stepfather snorted. "He ain't said nothin' about anything since I moved in here."

Mrs. Evans pushed a pan to the back of the stove and began to untie her apron. "Now hold on," her husband snapped. "I got to have breakfast before I go to town. Nothin' we can do now, anyway. If Cliff hadn't been so dumb, he'd have told us he didn't feel good."

After school, I sat in the office and stared blankly at the records spread out before me. I was to read the file and write the obituary for the school paper. The almost bare sheets mocked the effort. Cliff Evans, white, never legally adopted by stepfather, five young half-brothers and sisters. These meager strands of information and the list of "D" grades were all the records had to offer.

Cliff Evans had silently come in the school door in the mornings and gone out the school door in the evenings, and that was all. He had never belonged to a club. He had never played on a team. He had never held an office. As far as I could tell, he had never done one happy, noisy kid thing. He had never been anybody at all.

How do you go about making a boy into a zero? The grade school records showed me. The first- and second-grade teachers' annotations read, "Sweet, shy child," "timid, but eager." Then the third grade note had opened the attack. Some teacher had written in a good, firm hand, "Cliff won't talk. Uncooperative. Slow learner." The other academic sheep had followed with "dull," "slow-witted," "low I.Q." They became correct. The boy's I.Q. score in the ninth grade was listed at 83. But his I.Q. in the third grade had been 106. The score didn't go under 100 until the seventh grade. Even the shy, timid, sweet children have resilience. It takes time to break them.

I stomped to the typewriter and wrote a savage report pointing out what education had done to Cliff Evans. I slapped a copy on the principal's desk and another in the sad, dog-eared file. I banged the typewriter and slammed the file and crashed the door shut, but I didn't feel much better. A little boy kept walking after me, a little boy with a peaked, pale face; a skinny body in faded jeans; and big eyes that had looked and searched for a long time and then had become veiled.

I could guess how many times he had been chosen last to play sides in a game, how many whispered child conversations had excluded him, how many times he hadn't been asked. I could see and hear the faces that said over and over, "You're nothing, Cliff Evans."

A child is a believing creature. Cliff undoubtedly believed them. Suddenly, it seemed clear to me: When finally there was nothing left at all for Cliff Evans, he collapsed on a snow bank and went away. The doctor might list "heart failure" as the cause of death, but that wouldn't change my mind.

We couldn't find 10 students in the school who had known Cliff well enough to attend the funeral as his friends. So the student body officers and a committee from the junior class went as a group to the church, being politely sad. I attended the services with them and sat through it with a lump of cold lead in my chest and a big resolve growing through me.

I've never forgotten Cliff Evans or that resolve. He has been my challenge year after year, class after class. I look for veiled eyes or bodies scrounged into a seat in an alien world. "Look, kids," I say silently. "I may not do anything else for you this year, but not one of you is going to come out of here as a nobody. I'll work or fight to the bitter end doing battle with society and the school board, but I won't have one of you coming out of there thinking himself a zero."

Most of the time—not always, but most of the time—I've succeeded.

And then there was Don Cheney, a personal experience I will share with you.

Don Cheney (1941–1955)

I attended junior high school in a small Ohio town. In the 8th grade, one frosty Monday November morning, I came to school, and students in homeroom were already buzzing about Don Cheney. Seems his parents found him hanging in the family barn on Saturday morning, with a carefully made baling twine noose nailed into a rafter around his neck and a kicked-over stepladder underneath him.

"What's going on?" I said to my buddy Larry who sat behind me in homeroom.

"Don Cheney hung himself!" Larry exclaimed. "Didn't leave a note or nothin'!"

I can still remember my thoughts at the time. I ruminated to myself, Don Cheney. Don Cheney? Now who the heck was Don Cheney?

This is most remarkable since I had been in this school for 3 years with Don Cheney. There were only about 90 boys in the whole class of 1960, and he was in my cohort group homeroom!

"Which one was Don Cheney?" I asked Larry, looking around to see if I could discern who was missing. I couldn't.

"He was that white-headed kid—sat over there by the blackboard," Larry pointed to an empty chair along the sidewall.

I still couldn't quite place him.

Larry continued, "He was that quiet kid, the one that always ran by himself in PE." Bingo! Then I remembered him. When we ran laps in Frysinger's gym class, we always ran with a buddy to chat with—sometimes in little cliques of three or four. But Cheney always ran by himself in the back of the pack, never speaking to anyone.

I then remembered that I didn't even know the sound of his voice—and that's saying something for a male mid-kid. They usually can't shut up for more than a nanosecond!

But Don Cheney never said anything to anyone. He sat by himself in the cafeteria. All of our classes were together, and he never raised his hand in class to contribute, nor did he ever raise it to ask for help. He just sat along the side of the room and kept to himself.

Even in death, he kept it all quiet. No one ever knew why, on a bitterly cold Saturday morning, Don set his alarm extra early even for a farm kid, and all alone, this 14-year-old boy, wearing only a t-shirt, jeans, and tennis shoes, went out to the barn and hanged himself.

It haunts me to this day—almost 50 years later—as if it were yesterday.

Don Cheney will always be one of the posters in my head for Shadow Children.

You did not die in vain, Don.

Shadow Children, if noticed, are often classified by school systems as being *at risk*. They are not special education students and often do not have any of the alphabetic designations, such as LD, BD, ADD, or ADHD. The original label of *at risk* derived from students being seen as at risk of dropping out of school. Schools have rarely addressed the issue of students dropping out who were not identified as at risk prior to dropping out. These students had obviously been at risk, but no one noticed. The criteria were incorrect obviously.

Why wouldn't a school system, the center of *learning* in a community, be the first to learn from its own glaring miscalculation?

Many states and agencies have played with various definitions of the term *at risk*. Some districts use the term easily, others awkwardly, and some are in denial and have stated for the record that they do not have any at-risk students. One case I can think of is a high school with over 2,000 students, which claims it has no students who are at risk. This is despite the fact that they graduated 200 less seniors than their entering freshmen count 4 years previous. One might even call this practice "fudging," to be polite. As some school districts try to deny the existence of the Shadow Children or at least narrow the definition, others are fighting to bring the accurate count of at-risk youth into the light and even expand the definition.

The point of view of this book is that we need to find a way to answer two questions clearly:

1. How can you begin to know what you did not know? In other words, how can we begin to spot these students who are at risk of not succeeding in school and/or not succeeding in life *prior* to their becoming a statistic?
2. What prevention/intervention practices/programs should be instituted?

Let us begin to answer the first question by clearly defining what we mean by *at risk* and what the lead-ups are to becoming at risk.

Later, we will then look at the means by which we can educationally intervene and deliberately and consistently save these children and give them a life commensurate with the American Dream.

CHAPTER 5

Expanding the Definition of at Risk:
Are You Crazy?

I am the Director of the National At-Risk Education Network (NAREN). I receive no salary for this job. I tell you these things because I want you to know that my motives in what I am about to say are child-centered. I believe in every fiber of my being that we have the answers to make the difference needed to save many at-risk children from a certain fate of poverty and pain. NAREN stands for many principles, one of which is the expansion of the definition of what the term at risk means. Not only is NAREN interested in examining the substantial issue of dropout prevention, but it is also examining quality of life issues as well. Equally important is the moving away from a narrow focus on characteristics of children and broadening the view to include the school *within* the definition.

Typically, I am met with incredulity when I share the idea of definition expansion with people. They say in effect, "If we cannot meet the needs of this population by the narrower traditional definition, wouldn't it be insane to expand it, thereby basically creating a still larger population whose needs we cannot address?" At first glance, this certainly appears to be so, if one is taking a linear and logical view of things.

But if there is one thing we have learned, it is that most people, and certainly at-risk children, are neither linear nor logical. Educators who have not yet learned this are soaked in daily frustration with their clientele, wondering, "what is wrong with these children?" Nothing. Nothing is wrong with them, except that they just do not measure up to erroneously drawn expectations—expectations that are still based on the old scope and sequence way of thinking about curriculum and the people it is *intended* to fit.

This discrepancy between expectations and reality is even more extreme when dealing with Shadow Children. Most at-risk children are whole-to-part learners. Schools are set up in a part-to-whole assembly line fashion, again assuming a linear logical philosophy. Our current definitions and modalities of instruction with at-risk kids are yesterday, so yesterday that we have further decreased the chance for at-risk children to succeed, making sure the Shadow Children stay in the shadows.

Some people wonder if, subconsciously, our real purpose is not to drive these kids out of schools entirely. If that is true, we need to wake up because, even if we would drive them out, where would they go? They would be in our communities, but now as undereducated, alienated adults raising yet another generation of school-haters. It is essential to look at our definitions, values, and approaches to reaching the at risk so that we can modernize our efforts and increase the success rate for these children. And, I believe, it is *the* humane thing to do.

Let's look more closely at the Shadow Children issue from this perspective of definitions. Definitions can be thought of as assessments in another form. They suggest a diagnosis of the problem and a listing of telltale symptoms. Of course, the major reason for clearly defining here is to suggest more precise avenues of remediation.

Therefore, to define the word *definition* for our paradigm of interest:

- a *bad* definition = an ineffective highway of remediation
- a *good* definition = an effective highway of remediation

Old Definitions

Listed below are some of the usual and customary definitions of at risk:

AT-RISK is:
Chronic absenteeism and truancy from school
Chronic behavior problems
Chronic underachievement in school
Family illiteracy
Physical/sexual/psychological abuse
Cultural differences

Ethnic or racial differences
Social/developmental immaturity
Substance abuse
Limited English proficiency
Lacks occupational goals/skills
Chronic health problems
—Utah Gov. Dept. of Workforce Services

In the eyes of area service providers, of the one million children (infants to 18 years) who live in Harris County at least one third are at-risk simply because they live in poverty. Risk factors range from drug use and failure in school to gang violence, abuse, learning disabilities, limited language skills and neglect.
—Houston, Texas, Youth Services of Harris Co.

At-Risk means pupils in grades 5 to 12 who are at risk of not graduating from high school because they failed the high school graduation test, are dropouts, or are two or more of the following:

1. One or more years behind their age group in the number of high school credits attained.
2. Two or more years behind their age group in basic skill levels.
3. Habitual truants.
4. Parents.
5. Adjudicated delinquents.
6. Eighth grade pupils whose score in each subject area on the 8th grade examination was below basic level, or who failed to be promoted to the ninth grade.

—Wisconsin Department of Public Instruction

These three references reflect an ingrained and dangerous bias. No kid ever asked to be placed at risk or aimed for it deliberately, yet these definitions treat them as if they chose these traits. In order to reverse this old-fashioned and detrimental defining, we must stop looking solely at kids' characteristics as a definition of at risk and look at the partner in the dance of at-riskness, *the school*. Some will want to shy away from this angle of vision because, at first glance, once again, the school looks at fault, and the rejoinder arises that everyone knows, "We are doing the best we can with the little money we have."

New Definitions, New Ways

If education refuses to change its definition, then we are left in the very lame position of responding to their presence sounding something like, "Until these children rid themselves of their characteristics, we cannot do much for them." This leaves us educators looking hopeless and helpless, and I maintain that the *last* thing Shadow Children need are hopeless and helpless people in charge of their most formative years. If we accept NAREN'S definition of at risk, we find more effective empowerment for the school because it shows us the potential areas of impact where the school *can* do something.

> *At-risk student* means: Students may be at-risk when they experience a significant mismatch between their circumstances and needs, and the capacity or availability of appropriate educational opportunities which accommodate and respond to those students circumstances and needs in a manner that supports and enables their maximum social, emotional, and intellectual growth and development.
> —National At-Risk Education Network

The NAREN definition allows and encourages the school to assess all children under their care to ascertain if indeed they are at risk and then to design a compensatory program (that may or may not include academic emphasis).

The strong implication of this definition is that, as long as you have at-risk students, the school is part of the problem, as well as the solution.

The old, outmoded definition of at risk reminds me of my work in the South during school integration issues in the late 1960s when some thought it was enough to have *equal opportunity* for children being bussed to achieve racially mixed schools. It wasn't. It helped, but it wasn't nearly enough. The children might have those new books and better teachers in the new school, but the children were *not ready* for those books, and the teachers were *not ready* for the students in many ways.

It was not until the Federal government added the phrase *of attainment* that the school began to do more than just slap the new book in front of African American children and say, "There! Now you have the new book—read it!" Once the complete formula for compensatory education was stated as *equal opportunity of attainment*, the school had to own up to the fact that they must make a genuine effort to reach the students where they were—not demand that they stretch to a level they didn't have the skills to reach. At-risk kids often need the same prescription for school success: *equal opportunity of attainment*.

Larger Definitions

Not only do we need more depth in the definition of at risk, but also more breadth. NAREN accepts dropout behavior(s) as a legitimate *half* of the definition and expands it laterally by adding *being at risk of not succeeding in life because of being raised in unfavorable circumstances.* This begs us as professional educators to look at the symptomologies of students coming from dysfunctional situations and understand and have compassion for them and not punish, shame, or deny them our help because they are sporting survivor symptoms in a frequently unpleasant package. Imagine a medical doctor refusing treatment because you have a bad attitude with regard to your cancer symptoms!

We will look at this second half of the expanded defintion of at-risk Shadow Children in Section II.

Conclusion

We must stretch to a new level of professionalism. We must look at different standards and definitions for at-risk education, standards and defintions that are research-based and needs-based just for at-risk students, standards and definitions that value students who never asked to be placed at-risk and who look to us to coach them out of their dilemma, not punish them for finding themselves in that dilemma equipped with few, if any, skills to find their own way.

> To ask at-risk kids to be better than their parents is asking them to be heroes. Very few of us are heroes.
>
> —Jerry Conrath, author *Early Prevention*

The NAREN contention is that if we expand and deepen the definition and officially meet some of the nonacademic needs of Shadow Children, we may very well find the population defined by the old definitions dropping in numbers, rather than dropping out.

CHAPTER 6

Counting the Shadow Children—Part I

The Dropout Scenario

THE question from the media often is, "Is the at-risk student population increasing, or staying the same, or decreasing?"

Often, a complicated question is disguised as a simple one. This is one of those. If one wanted a sound-bite answer to this question, as most media people do, it would be meaningless. This may be why many educational issues discussed in the media *are* often meaningless, trivialized, and/or incoherent and misleading.

Let me emphasize that whether the at-risk population is increasing or decreasing is a most serious question. It is a critical question because counts determine funding and programming, and more often than not, outcomes depend on proper funding and programming. Sometimes counts are about where a new highway should be routed or where a new hamburger place will be located. Counts mean something to the people involved, but not much to the rest of us. Highways are everywhere. Hamburgers are too. But dealing with funding and programming for at-risk children is often going to be a matter of life or death to those children. It is as serious as a suicide or a life of poverty.

Someone meddling with the count of the bank drawer goes to jail—over a paper substance called dollars. Someone meddling with the count of Shadow Children gets—nothing. Nothing happens as a result. Nothing, except that kids who desperately need help and look to the authorities in education to support and defend them are denied that help and continue their downward spiral into merely statistical significance.

Count *is* important. Let's look closely at the issue. It is complex, but understandable. In order to meaningfully answer the question whether the number of at-risk students is increasing or decreasing in the United States, one has to carefully define parameters.

The concept of the *at-risk student count* is quite amorphous, and this has helped it become a "chameleon" statistic in educational political arenas. The figures that hit the media often have been filtered and spun to place the agency releasing the figures in the best possible light. National political parties, during their own administrations, will focus only on the statistics that work for them. What makes their party look good and what makes the other party or opponent look bad? Many people expect this statistical coloring among politicians, but shamefully, school administrators use these tactics as well.

Using the confusion and cloudiness created by various and poor definitions, school administrators who will be penalized for having large populations of at-risk kids are able to find ways to underreport those figures. State departments of education know this and laugh about it, but then enable it by both failing to establish a clear definition as to specifically what *at risk* means and by not imposing any penalties whatsoever upon local districts that make false reports.

If you do not confront, you enable.

Why would a state department of education enable something as serious as misidentifying a population that is in such desperate need of assistance? Let us answer that by asking two questions:

1. How does it reflect upon a state department of education when its state's at-risk figures are higher than neighboring states?
2. What economic fallout is there for a state when its Shadow Children statistics impact the possibility of new industry locating within its borders?

The bottom line can often be the dollar, not the needs of kids. "Follow the money" is the appropriate rejoinder if you want answers to why we have not done a better job of solving our at-risk students' needs and why convenient confusion is allowed (or encouraged) to remain. Of course, the end result is a conspiracy, whether conscious or unconscious, to push the Shadow Children further into the shadows.

So, with all that being said, several angles of view need to be shared in order to answer the increase/decrease question. The actual count will primarily be determined by definition and, secondly, by effective data gathering. Honesty in reporting will be the third factor.

Defining Dropout

First, some people/agencies define at risk only as at risk of dropping out of school, but even this very narrow definition does not provide as much comfort as one might think. There are actually four (4) ways of defining what only seems like a solid statistic based on a clear head count.

1. *Event Dropout Rate:* the percentage of students who drop out of school in a given year
2. *Status Dropout Rate:* the percentage of young people (usually 16–24 years old) who are not currently enrolled in school and who do not have a diploma or GED
3. *High School Completion Rate:* the complement of the status dropout rate (1 minus the status dropout rate) but based on 18–24 year olds, not on 16–18 year olds
4. *Promoting Power:* the ratio of the number of students in a certain grade to the number that graduate when expected to graduate

Statistics are often warped by including GED recipients as graduates, and research shows clearly that a GED *is not* the equivalent of a high school diploma by any stretch in terms of social acceptance or, perhaps more importantly, economic gain for the recipient. Some research shows that the very existence of the GED increases drop-out figures [Greene, 2002, p. 23].

One does not expect the general public to know of all these definitions, although the impact of the differences is tremendous. A NAREN survey of over 400 teachers has found that *not a single one* knew these definitional categories existed, much less the impact created by varying the selection of a particular definition. That is reprehensible professional naiveté. Why? Because it becomes part of the unconscious conspiracy against children who need support. Unfortunately, ignorance can kill just as well as a cold-hearted, deliberate murderer.

There appears to be enough confusion and chaos without even looking at the much larger definition of *at-risk youth* as espoused by NAREN and laid out in the previous chapter. But going by the figures we do currently have and generously assuming that the figures reported by schools are even close to accurate, we at least have the first answer to the increase/decrease question.

Statistically Significant Indicator #1

While dropout rates for non-Hispanic whites and blacks have declined substantially (from 12 to 7 percent and 21 to 13 percent, respectively) between 1972 and 2000, there was no statistically significant decline among Hispanics. Twenty-eight percent of Hispanic young adults drop out before completing school. This is a tragic figure.

The final sound-bite answer here within this set of dropout count parameters would be: Things are better for Whites and Blacks; no change for Hispanics.

[By the way, if you're wondering which of the four definitions of dropouts this sound bite answer is based on, it's: *The Status Dropout Rate*.]

So, to refresh your memory: Students may be at risk when they experience a significant mismatch between their circumstances and needs, and the capacity or availability of appropriate educational opportunities that accommodate and respond to them in a manner that supports and enables their maximum social, emotional, and intellectual growth and development. Again, this involves the school inside the definition, rather than outside the definition. If the Shadow Child has these *other* statistics against him or her [poverty, Alcohol and Other Drug Addiction (AODA), teen pregnancy, emotional issues, etc.) and the school cannot accommodate those symptomatic behaviors, then the school falls down and literally becomes part of the problem. With this in mind, the answer to the increase/decrease question is: The number of Shadow Children is *increasing*.

Statistically Significant Indicator #2

Following a substantial increase in participation between 1996 and 1999, the proportion of pre-kindergarten 3- to 5-year-olds attending center-based early childhood care and education programs dropped from 60 percent to 56 percent in 2001.

Why is this a problem? In 1990, the National Education Goals Panel established its first National Education Goal: "By the year 2000, all children in America will start school ready to learn." To reach this goal, the Goals Panel created three objectives for families and communities, the first of which stated that "all children will have access to high-quality and developmentally appropriate preschool programs that help prepare children for school." The Goals Panel also designated preschool participation, particularly by children living in poverty, as an indicator of progress toward this goal.

We are clearly failing here, and the eventual payoff will be disastrous because there will be a ballooning statistical cluster of children beginning school with low readiness skills—entering schools already having difficulty dealing with special needs in children. Based on statistically significant indicator #2, the answer would be: The number of Shadow Children is *increasing*.

It's clearly a pay me now or pay me later scenario, but the delayed payment will be much costlier. Meanwhile, children are suffering and officials underreporting or fudging figures are taking liberal license with those lives. Each time this inaccurate reporting occurs, inefficiency and/or incompetency is covered up at the expense of accurate data that is critical to effective planning, funding, and programming for Shadow Children who desperately need it. If we define crime as harming the innocent, then the practice of deliberately misreporting could be interpreted as a criminal offense.

Section II

Shadow Children Also Develop from a Bad Start

CHAPTER 7

Counting the Shadow Children—Part II

At Risk of Not Succeeding in Life

WE have a plethora of figures showing that if you drop out of school, it has lifelong economic impact. This is no small matter; money is important. Money is a means to many ends: better nutrition, better health care, better housing, better education, better and safer neighborhoods, better clothing, and more, all bearing on the freedom to choose a longer and healthier life. No money, few choices. More money, more choices. More education/more money does not mean a person *will* choose those things that promote a longer healthier life, but they will at least have the opportunity to choose those things. Education is about opportunity, more doors of opportunity to open as opposed to having just one or, perhaps, no door of opportunity.

Dropping out of school is not a choice we should allow. We no longer allow children to choose to drink or smoke. Why? Because drinking or smoking has life-damaging consequences that children cannot foresee. So we make that decision for them. Adults get the freedom to self-destruct if they want to, supposedly because they can see the consequences of their actions. Children, as a rule, cannot see the consequences of their actions, so we assume *in loco parentis* powers and make laws to protect children from themselves. Dropping out of education is proven, beyond a shadow of a doubt, to have life-damaging consequences. We should never allow children to drop out of school. The data and stories to support such prohibition are abundant.

The second part of the new definition of Shadow Children is that they are at risk of not succeeding in life. Just why is NAREN so aggressively seeking this expansion to the old narrow definition?

Several years ago, a national speaker at a conference ended his lecture to a group of educators of at-risk students with this statement: "Doctors know why they are in business. Ministers know why they are in business. Dentists know why they are in business. Why is it that, in our profession, educators are so confused about what business we are in? Isn't that a shame?" I looked around at the other educators in my immediate area with a raised eyebrow. Seemed to me we *did* know what business we were in. But just in case the speaker was right for some educators, let me set the record straight about what our business is: *We are in the SUCCESS business!*

Doctors promote people's physical health. Dentists promote people's oral health. Ministers promote people's spiritual health. And we educators? *We promote and nurture children's ability to succeed in life.* Isn't this clear to us? I hope so. But maybe it isn't. Maybe we want to stay confused so we can't feel the sting of the obvious message that, if we are in the success business and the kids (our clientele) are failing, we are obviously failing.

Q: What is your business?
A: I sell cars. I am a car salesman.

Q: How many buyers do you have?
A: Well, I don't have any buyers.

Q: Well then, how can you be a salesman?
A: Gosh, now that you put it that way, I guess I am not a salesman yet.

If we educators are in the success business, then we had better start defining ourselves by that standard. And, if a chain is as strong as its weakest link, is it not true that: *A school is as good as its worst students.*

If we are in the success business and just a few of our students spend years in our programs and *still* do not succeed, what does that say about us?

If Jim makes 100 contacts with potential buyers and sells no cars, he is no salesman. If Sally makes 100 contacts with potential buyers and sells 100 cars, she is substantially better than Jim.

Q: What does Jim with zero sales say when he hears about Sally's 100 sales?

1. Wow, Sally is getting better clients than I do. It has nothing to do with me.
2. Clients are not what they used to be.
3. This place sucks. I'm glad vacation is coming because I need it.
4. I have a lot to learn obviously. Maybe Sally will show me how she reaches her clients more effectively than I do.

What should we say to ourselves as professionals when we discover that some of our students are not succeeding in life after spending 12 of their most formative years with us for the express purpose of success preparation?

Youth at Risk from a Bad Start

Talk to any experienced elementary teacher, and she/he will tell you that they can spot at-risk children easily in the K–3 grades. Most all of these children come from homes of poverty, neglect, and/or abuse. This should not be a revelation to anyone.

Facts we know:

- Over 1,000,000 of the 3,092,000 children reported for child abuse and neglect to CPS agencies are verified in the United States each year, and one can only guess how many go unreported or are true but lack verification. Without a doubt, the actual numbers of abused and neglected children are much higher.
- 13,500,000 children live in poverty—about one in five (18.9 percent).
- 512,000 babies are born to teen mothers each year.
- 2,100,000 children are arrested each year.
- An estimated 1,600,000 children in the United States have an imprisoned father, and 200,000 have an imprisoned mother. Most children with incarcerated parents live in poverty before, during, and after their parents' incarceration.
- In 1999, 26 percent of 12th graders, 22 percent of 10th graders, and 12 percent of 8th graders had used illicit drugs in the previous 30 days.

- In 1999, 31 percent of 12th graders, 26 percent of 10th graders, and 15 percent of 8th graders reported having five or more alcoholic beverages in a row in the previous 2-week period.
- Every 5 hours in the United States, another youth commits suicide. Besides the tragic loss of another young individual, the act of suicide itself devastatingly impacts dozens of friends and relatives left behind.

All the children included in the above statistics (and more categories not listed) come to school carrying their burdens and issues with them. It is safe to assume that many of the children represented in the above figures are, indeed, at risk of having decreased horizons of success. By default, our schools have become the focus of efforts to address serious issues of Shadow Children. Schools readily admit they are both inadequately informed and inadequately prepared for this immense task, but this has not stopped many of them from making the noble effort.

The War We Are In

The Angel-Warrior At-Risk Educator Code

We literally are in a war to save many of our children. Our enemies are many. Our first goal is to gain clarity about our goals. The clarity certainly includes knowing our enemies, the first of which is *ignorance*.

How Do We Arm Ourselves?

1. We must develop an unbridled, unstoppable, impassioned, intelligent, and persistent effort to lower these figures in any way we can, child by child.
2. We must develop an internal locus of control for ourselves and seek out other colleagues and interested citizens who are determined to proactively make a difference.
3. We must learn about Shadow Children, their academic, psychological, and social issues, and their individual learning needs and styles.
4. We must get serious about the education of Shadow Children, not

only with the daily classroom interface, but also comprehensively, pre-K–12 and beyond.

5. We must be the champions to children that they need in order to develop healthfully. We need to get close to them, rather than turn away; talk to them about important things in their lives, rather than ignore them; and let them know we care, rather than act like we wish they would disappear.

6. In other words, we need to embrace these children and clearly send the message that we *want* them, *need* them, and above all, *love* them.

This book has been written to help arm educational stakeholders with the knowledge necessary to provide the avenues of liberation Shadow Children need.

It is a glorious war we are in—it is all about the things of which great fiction are often made, only this is very real. It is about rescuing the helpless, rooting out decay, and replacing it with marvelous life enhancements. It often comes down to good triumphing over some form of evil. It is about saving lives. What could be more exciting or worthwhile than that? How many professionals get the chance to be dedicated to such a worthy cause?

Unfortunately, it is often a thankless job, with long unbroken stretches of solitary work. As service workers, we must sustain ourselves sometimes, but we must also make the effort and time to network with our colleagues, not only to share information that might expedite our work, but also to inspire one another with our hope, strength, and experience.

Above all, we must be courageous, intelligent, and persistent angel-warrior educators.

CHAPTER 8

Understanding the Effects
of Abuse and Neglect

F REEDOM of choice is power. Shadow Children, many of whom are survivors of dysfunctional families, are often raised in ignorance, and they become shackled by that ignorance—ignorance about emotions, relationships with others and self, limits and boundaries, and other essential tools and skills necessary for a thriving life. This ignorance—again, one of our main enemies in this battle—leaves survivors with limited choices and, therefore, limited power. Their universe has been artificially restricted by unenlightened caregivers who, perhaps unintentionally, have constricted to a mere slice what life has to offer Shadow Children and who, without intervention, they will have to offer back to the world.

This book is not about building yet another case about what trouble our youth is in or laying blame here and there. I think most people know by now that it is society's/parents'/the media's/the school's/God's/poor nutrition and allergies' fault. Enough grousing, whimpering, carping, and other sounds have been done, and still the problems exist in record numbers.

Q: Why have we not been able to make a substantial dent in these horrifying statistics?

A: We have failed to understand the psychological and societal dynamics that birth these problems again and again.

Q: What do we need to know?

A: We need to thoroughly understand the vulnerable attack points of these issues.

Q: Who needs this understanding?

A: Educators and educational stakeholders—all those desiring to be specially prepared champions of our children.

Q: What forms of understanding would be most useful?

A: We need teachers fortified with the techniques, processes, practices, and programs that will and can be used to specifically benefit our youth, regardless of age level or content area. We need stakeholders sharing their time, resources, ideas, and enthusiastic support.

This section of the book is a concentrated focusing onto the effects of abuse within and around the victim. The concern is not with blame but, instead, with the dynamics of abuse and neglect, their aftereffects, and how, once started, these *dynamics* develop an identity of their own. This identity, known here as the Shadow Child Syndrome, impacts both the victim's life and the lives of those around the victim. The impact of this intra- and interpersonal virus is deadening at best and deadly at worst. It is so critical that we understand the dynamics of the long-term effects of abuse and neglect that we must temporarily suspend our concerns with fault-finding, social implications, and litigation issues. In this way, we can impartially and objectively see what lies behind the veil of this virulent syndrome.

In our world today, there appears to be more protection for perpetrating adults than for their helpless victims, especially when the abuser is a parent. It is incredible that we still find a "children-as-chattel" mentality surviving to the detriment of our children's welfare. The goal herein is to disseminate a psychodynamic understanding of the consequences of abuse and neglect. With such understanding we can better focus our resources to more effectively champion children.

There are those who deny the need for understanding dysfunctional family survivor dynamics, usually while carefully tending their own symptoms. Some of us wonder what keeps these fellow human beings so blind to their own condition, often appearing righteous in their misery. Some call it arrogance; some call it denial. It is as if they are incapable of seeing the impact of such devastation in their own and others' lives: "Yes, I'm miserable. There may or may not be help, but I'm not going to avail myself of it." Perhaps this section can help remove the blinders of denial. There is much to gain, namely freedom and power, and little to lose, except for old pain and the fatigue of carrying around heavy and unnecessary baggage that should have been dropped long ago.

Survivors of abuse and neglect eventually manifest what is termed the Shadow Children Syndrome. There are several chapters dedicated to exploring the implications of the syndrome and how they bring those symptoms to school. Within the framework provided by this book's purposes is also a proposed nomenclature of abuse and neglect, so the reader can become familiar with the forms of abuse. It's not fun reading, but if you want to recognize trouble when you see it, you have to see it in advance. Oncologists must become familiar with cancer before they see it in a patient if they are to be effective in bringing about a cure. Educators, likewise, may have to look at some forms of abuse to know it when they see it. More in-depth coverage and resources are found in the bibliography.

There is some unpleasant truth in this book. Fortunately, the flipside of this information is that it allows one to do something about the burdensome baggage. Internalizing the information in this book can help the individual avoid denial, the carrier of all dysfunctionality, and can facilitate effective intervention to put an end to what often becomes a vicious cycle of abuse and neglect.

CHAPTER 9

Dysfunctionality

THE word *dysfunctional* may be descriptive, but it is limiting because it sounds like broken or damaged goods. Many people automatically think the word refers to the most degenerative of families, but it applies in some ways to a majority of families. A critic of what was at one time faddishly called the Adult Child Movement sarcastically exclaimed, "Why don't you just say that anybody with less than perfect parents becomes an Adult Child?" Tongue-in-cheek or not, this is a fairly accurate statement. Almost anyone with less than perfect parents as a child can have unfinished business as an adult and on the road to becoming an adult. The further from perfect your parents were (in other words, the more noncherishing moments you had as a child), the more unfinished business you can have as an adult. Recovery is not a matter of defending or blaming parents (although this may be a stage some adults need to work through) but is, rather, a matter of taking responsibility for getting on with life. Getting on with life may necessitate figuring out what is lacking in one's toolbox of life skills because of those historical deprivations and then doing some compensatory work—work well worth the effort if one believes that daily vitality is a desirable goal.

It is perhaps best to think of functionality on a scale from low to high. The notion that all families can be divided into just the two categories of functional and dysfunctional is dualistic and, therefore, overly simplistic and misleading. Most families have moments of high functionality, as well as moments of low functionality. The higher the proportion of low-functioning moments (episodes of abuse and neglect) to high-functioning moments (episodes of affirmation and nurturance) during child-raising years, the more the possibility of unfinished business for the individual in his/her development.

Another factor that must be considered is the level of traumatization created within the individual. This is a mysterious and extremely individualistic factor. Some children walk away from trauma unscathed. Some people walk away apparently unscathed, only to discover later that they had unconsciously repressed or consciously suppressed the effects of the trauma. When the effects of trauma are buried, they often surface later in life. We call this usually unwelcome surfacing *activation*. Sometimes the activation is obviously related to historical abuse and neglect, but more often, it exhibits itself in a nonstraightforward manner, as described in the eight characteristics of the Shadow Child Syndrome and in Chapter 13 about implications of the syndrome for educators. Once a child gets activated, they may "act out" with behaviors that help provide some release from the pressure of emotional activation. An example of this is a child who was sexually abused becoming promiscuous whenever she/he experiences feelings of shame. The feeling of shame is activation, and the promiscuity is the acting out as a subconscious means to reduce the pressure of this powerful emotion.

Of course, some people don't walk away from trauma at all, and it is quite apparent that they have been damaged, perhaps in many ways, by what has happened to them. Psychiatric hospitals, doctors' offices, and prisons are full of these victims exhibiting unfinished business, each in their own way. As the Berlin Wall was a constant reminder of just how terrible Communism could be, so are the painful statistics of our institutions a constant monument to the cruelty against children. The righteousness exhibited by the abusers, neglectors, and their enablers will never be sufficient to camouflage the glaring statistics of our health and penal institutions, which are filled with survivors of abuse and neglect. Perhaps the silenced voices of those who did not survive should be the loudest testimony of all.

Functional vs. Dysfunctional

There has always been heated debate over what a functional family is or is not. We are going to clear that up here. One thing we can say is that a functional family is *not* dysfunctional. What is meant by this is that a functional family is not abusive or neglectful. The Classification

System of Child Abuse and Neglect (CSCAN) classification tables in Appendix I make clear what behaviors are abusive/neglectful.

What also obfuscates a clear-cut definition in our modern society is that who or what constitutes a family can often be quite amorphous. In reality, there is no such thing as a family. There is a collection of individuals to whom we attach the name *family*. Individuals are changing each minute. One need only reflect upon oneself. We change moods, needs, thoughts, words, and behaviors constantly. How would one clearly define what a person is? We would say people vary, or the definition depends on when you take a snapshot view of an individual. One minute they are this, and the next minute they are that. Multiply this across how many persons are in this collective thing labeled *family* and grasp the difficulty in clearly defining what a family is. It changes from minute to minute just as the people in it constantly change.

One must feel a bit of empathy for the Census Bureau as they try to compose a questionnaire so effective that everyone can put themselves into the right box when it comes to the family category. This is probably why they finally settled for the term *household*. How many people live in the apartment or house that you own or for which you pay rent? Asking the question that way gets them off the hook. And if the Census Bureau cannot figure out what a family is, how is the ordinary citizen to figure it out? We just assume that all families are like *our* family. They are not. Families are hugely different from one another, and their effects on the children are hugely different as well.

One way to think of a family is like that of an assembly line. General Motors brings their raw material, parts, tools, workers and designs to the beginning of the assembly line, and they do not expect a Ford to pop out at the end. At the end of the assembling process, they get what they put into the assemblage all the way down the line. It is not much different with families. Submitting developing children to abuse and neglect and expecting loving, caring, healthy young adults to pop out at the end is delusional. The Ward Cleaver/Bill Cosby family is long gone. How gone is it?

1. Divorce rates in the United States are now at 50 percent.
2. Unmarried women commonly bear and rear 33 percent of the nation's children.
3. If there are two parents in the home, dual career parents are the norm.

4. Only 30 percent of families have a biological parent working at home and the other in a career outside the home (Weissberg et al., 2003).

What do the statistics say about the state of kids today (in addition to the alarming stats in Chapter 1)?

1. One of every five children experiences symptoms of a mental disorder during the course of any one year. Less than 25 percent of these children receive appropriate services. (But they still come to school!) (Surgeon General's Report).

2. 30 percent of 14–17 year olds engage in multiple high-risk behaviors in any one year, and another 35 percent are considered medium-risk, being involved with one or two problem behaviors (Dryfoos).

3. 17.2 percent of U.S. children lived in poverty in 2002. This figure represents 12,423,000 children, an increase of 700,000 over the previous year (U.S. Census Bureau, 2004).

4. There are approximately 59,000,000 children in K–12 schools in the United States today. Over the last 30 years, the non-Hispanic White population has declined 16 percent, from 79 percent to 63 percent. The African American population in schools has increased 2 percent, from 14 percent to 16 percent. The Hispanic population has increased from 6 percent to 15 percent. The Asian and Pacific Islander population has expanded from 1 percent to 5 percent (U.S. Census Bureau, 2004). The dropout rate for Hispanics is 37 percent, compared to 18 percent for African Americans and 10 percent for Whites.

5. Drug, alcohol, and tobacco usage is increasing in teenagers: Nearly one-fourth, or 24 percent, of teenagers reported using illegal drugs (marijuana, cocaine, heroin, hallucinogens, and others) at least once in the 2002–2003 school year, compared with 22 percent the year before. Cigarette use increased slightly to 27 percent in the 2002–2003 school year, up from 26 percent the year before. Underage drinking is consistent: 50 percent of teens drink alcohol illegally (2002–2003 Pride Surveys).

Many of these statistics (and those in Chapter 1) have been a result of family dysfunction. So, maybe it is time now for us to clearly see the difference between

Functional ↔ Dysfunctional

The format of X vs. Y is useful for bringing distinctive and crystal clarity to the issue once and for all as to what differentiates a functional from a dysfunctional family.

Unfortunately, such dualistic formats can also be misleading. As was mentioned before, families are dynamic and ever changing. To statically call a family functional or another family dysfunctional might make for engaging journalism but in reality, at any moment in time, one family could suddenly shift categories. Sometimes even the best (most functional) of families fall apart under pressure and do something they later regret. Or sometimes it just cannot be helped. The story is told of Picasso's family, often represented as a most functional and, therefore, loving family, basically coming unglued during a series of horrendous earthquakes that hit Malaga, Spain, when Picasso was 3 years old. Hiding underground, his family was frantic and anxious to the point that, in front of little Pablo, Picasso's mother bore Picasso's sister Lola prematurely on a basement floor on Christmas Day. Not only did this affect Picasso and influence his painting, but his sister Lola became known affectionately as Little Earthquake to the family and friends who survived. In Picasso's famous painting "Guernica" we can see what might have happened in the mind of the 3-year-old child while he was watching the dying people and horses and listening to the children screaming for help on the long walk to the shelter (Miller, 1998). Suffice it to say that the past is truly not in the past. How much we carry with us into the future and how it affects us is determined by a mysterious equation based on factors in our vulnerability, our resiliency, and the failure of personal tools and coping skills to develop, which we need later in life.

After years of counseling work, research in the field of human psychology, and polling the best brains in the field of family systems, the NAREN staff proposes the following eight universal category continua for judging family health. It is based on how people in the family regard and treat one another. Most families probably fall somewhere in the middle of each pairing. It is not so much how family members act once in a while as it is what the *normed* behaviors are on a fairly constant basis.

Functional	Dysfunctional
• Affirms one another	• Critical of one another
• Refuses to abuse	• Righteously abuses
• Provides quality time	• Dedicated elsewhere
• Necessities provided	• Neglects basic needs
• Health needs met	• Health needs neglected
• Problems are opportunities	• Problems weaken
• It's OK to make mistakes	• Mistakes spotlighted/shamed
• Rides easy in the saddle	• Hypervigilance as a way of life

Affirmation

We all come into the world hardwired with the need for affection, nurturing, and cherishing, that is, affirmation in all of its forms. We are not preprogrammed for rejection, abuse, or neglect. When we run up against these experiences we find ways to cope and survive, but many of our coping attempts, despite being earnest, are warped reactions. We keep using them anyway.

Affirmation is a high form of human regard. The scale goes like this:

Intolerance → Tolerance → Acceptance → Affirmation

We are born ready for affirmation, meaning that we're ready to accept "I love you, applaud you, and value your uniqueness just the way you are." Intolerance is at the opposite end of affirmation, and it says to the child, "I detest you as you are; change or be in danger." Does a child know how to change in response to this? No, they just know how to *be*.

Tolerance says, in effect, "I don't really want you around, but the law [or culture, etc.] says I must put up with you. Don't expect me to like it or you."

Acceptance sounds nice, and it sure beats intolerance or mere tolerance, but it still shows a distance in a family—polite distance, but a distance never the less. "You are a child, and I cannot expect you to be anything else, just yet. But, thank goodness, someday you will grow up and not be such an acceptable bother."

Affirmation is wonderful. It is about wonderfulness. It says, in effect, "Wow! Some people from India are moving in next door. Cool! How long should I politely wait before I go over there and get to know them?"

Affirmation is unconditional approval of something or someone *exactly as they are*. Affirmation does not ask you to change but, rather, celebrates you and wishes there were more just like you. Affirmation is what infants come into the world expecting. Basically, infants expect a brass band in the delivery room, confetti, and long parades of applause and attention—and for it to never end. A family at its "most functional" should be like that: constantly affirming, regardless of whether you were born with a birth defect, don't sleep through the night for a year, or aren't the hoped for gender. We are not talking about preferring other behaviors. Sure, I would have preferred both my sons would have slept straight through every single night they went to bed, waking up only after I had brushed my teeth and had some coffee in the morning. I wish one of them had not almost scalped the cat with an enthusiastic grab or stuck a screwdriver into an electrical outlet (and twisted it). But these things they do are not *them*. They are behaviors I work to help them change, but I affirm their *essence*, what makes them the unique contribution to the world that they are. It is my privilege to know them, to learn from them, to work with them, and to laugh with them. I did not always do this well, but they were always treasured, and maybe that is a good synonym for affirmation.

Is this asking too much of a family? Of course not. If you are not prepared to affirm children, don't have one because, if children are not affirmed, they act out, and things get very confusing from then on. Kids do not need confusion; they need clear affirmation and direction. They need surety and confidence. Parents alone have this responsibility, and if they fail, the resulting symptomatic behaviors in children, in all the color and variety imaginable, quite often come to school with the child, creating chaotic and obstructive situations in what is supposed to be a learning environment.

Refusal to Abuse

Functional families are not a bunch of goofy Pollyannas. They know what each other's weaknesses are, what the fears are, what the vulnerabilities are, but they refuse to take advantage of them. They love one another too much to inflict deliberate harm. They also may be smart enough to realize that the payoff is not worth the activity; that is it is a bad investment of behavior. I tease you about the shape of your nose; then you cry, and we spend *all* kinds of time reassuring you that you are okay, apologizing, and trying to set things right—so why waste energy doing it in the first place when it is going to waste so much energy cleaning up after it?

Dysfunctional families look for opportunities to abuse. They think it fun in some instances, or their right in others, to hurt someone small and defenseless. They often misinterpret the Bible itself to justify doing so, such as quoting, "Spare the rod and spoil the child." Interestingly, hitting children for their own good actually is not what that statement means. In the Aramaic translation, the translation written most closely to the time of Christ, the rod was the shepherd's crook and symbolically represented giving love and protection, rather than using it to inflict pain. People who hit children are either cowards (they know they can get away with it because kids are smaller than they are) or ignorant (because there is no research at all that says it is good for children to be hit, but there is plenty that shows the damage that can be done) or are so full of anger they cannot help themselves and, therefore need therapy, or any and all combinations of the three.

In his book, *People of the Lie*, Dr. M. Scott Peck (1983), pitches a case for a new classification in the DSM (Diagnostic and Statistic Manual of Mental Disorders) for a category of *evil*. He is not talking about a religious issue. He is making a case for righteous and deliberate abuse to be seen as an official mental malady titled *evil* so that it can be recognized and treated. In light of this category of functional familyism, Peck's argument makes perfect sense. Shouldn't we be more concerned about this as a category than, say, nervous tics or obsessive hand washing, which do have special classifications? I am not belittling the need for treatment of nervous tics or compulsive rituals, but I am stating that people deliberately and righteously inflicting harm on others in and of itself certainly should be enough justification for a category.

Quality Time

Human energy is measured in time. Being alive means being in motion, that is, *doing* something, and we measure that doing by time. What did you do today? Well, I spent 20 minutes folding clothes, an hour going to the grocery, 8 hours sleeping, 42 minutes eating, and so on. That is how we measure our energy. Raising healthy children, tending a family effectively takes a lot of time—rather large chunks of time dedicated to maintenance, affection, fun, health, safety, and more.

If I walked up to you on the street and said, "Hey, could you give me about 40 hours a week of your time?" you would say, "What? Are you crazy? I am too busy. I can't find 3 hours a week to get in my 30-minute walking program. How am I supposed to give you 40 hours! You're nuts!" But people start children without ever considering this major contingency. And you must find the time because you are going to be spending at least 40 hours a week to raise that child up to adulthood—IF you are to do a quality job. Somewhere in there you have to not just count the clothes-washing/meal-fixing things, but you have to build in quality time.

What is quality time? The answer depends on the ages of the individuals and cultural norms in a family, but what it does mean in terms of common characteristics is dedicated time, aware and involved connection with one another, healthy interaction, closeness, and warmth. You can see why sitting and watching television in the same room would rarely fit the definition. Just eating at the same table might not qualify. Driving somewhere in the same car might not count. The point is that quality time is meaningful and nurturing to everyone involved. This takes thought and sometimes skillful planning. How many parents do that?

Necessities Are Provided

Abraham Maslow, among others, has done a good job of telling us straight out that we need food, water, warmth, and air. When children do not get these items, it makes headlines because it is so alarming. Children going unfed for days or being kept in suffocating closets, cages, or basements is shocking to many of us in the United States. That people might have to go without fresh water or live in the cold for months or years in our country is unthinkable.

The more functional a family is, the more they don't just "put food on the table." They are also knowledgeable about healthy and appropriate nutrition, healthy water, and clean air and are invested in upgrading these necessities when possible.

Health Needs Are Met

Children are properly immunized, allergies are tested and checked, strong and healthy teeth and bones are invested in, safety needs are seen to, checkups are done regularly, and sex education is properly conducted.

The more functional a family is, the better they do these things. This is another reason why poverty is violence. When families are deprived economically, they often cannot afford the costs, transportation, or other resources in people or time that it takes to get these necessary needs met in a complete and appropriate fashion. Lots of cash does not mean that functionality will be automatic. Some well-to-do families can be just as neglectful as a family that lives with economic deprivation, but the odds are better that, if a family is economically well off, health needs of the children will get met.

Why is this important? First, if your body is in a suffering state, Maslow (1971) tells us that it is very difficult to pay attention to higher needs, such as achievement and creativity and being all that we can be (self-actualizing). One's attention first and foremost, naturally goes to the toothache, the skin rash, the hunger in the stomach, a less than desirable appearance again and again. You cannot muster the concentration long enough for developing oneself to make it pay off—and development takes persistence. It is hard to persist at anything other than seeking relief when one is unhealthy.

It sends a subtle message of love to children when they see parents going to the extra length it takes to make sure they are healthy. Children may not send thank-you notes to parents for getting them braces or making sure the vitamin bottle is always full, but subconsciously, it is noticed and catalogued and, over time, sends a clear signal of care and support, "You are more than worthy of my sacrifices for you." It builds an underlying confidence in children.

When well-cared children grow up they take care of their children the same way, establishing a healthy legacy of behaviors that are passed on. Healthy legacies in families are what build a strong country over time.

Problems Are Opportunities

Pertinent to this area of functionality, I witnessed two significant incidences within a week of each other that make the point perfectly. I could not have staged them for a movie director any better. Maybe these things happen because of coincidence, or perhaps I just notice them because I am a professor of learning psychology and a former psychotherapist.

The observational opportunity involved sitting in two different restaurants just a few days apart, but observing two similar situations that were handled very differently. Both involved a mom (there, but not part of the story), a dad, and a small daughter of about 4 years of age. I was eating alone nearby—typically with a fork in one hand and a journal in the other—but in perfect proximity to view all aspects of these parallel situations. Both little girls spilled their cups; one had juice in a small glass, the other milk. When the first little tyke spilled her juice, the father went ballistic. "Now look what you have done!" He frantically grabbed a napkin, his tense body language similar to a military general moving alarmingly to stop the accidentally pushed red button from starting certain nuclear war. His face scowled at the little girl, and he huffed and puffed like the whole evening had just been ruined and it was her fault for not yet having finer muscle control. The look on her face was one of shame—sucked back in, with her lip quivering and her eyes going blank, as she must have learned to do many times before.

In the second situation, when the little girl spilled her small red plastic cup of milk, the father calmly looked over as the little girl began to get upset and began to reassure her, "That's okay, honey. These things happen." He smiled and picked up two paper napkins and gave her one. "Let's clean it up together," and again, "It's okay, sweetheart; it's just a little accident. We will get you more milk." Every kid should have such a dad.

The child in the second incident was actually the only one upset, and the father showed his stripes by making it a learning incident in several ways. One lesson, the obvious, is that accidents happen. It is what you do after the accident that counts. Second, the dad showed what a functional parent does in times of stress: comforts and reassures. There are enough rough bumps in the road of life without a parent making more, by topping it off with a clear message, "If you can't count on me when you spill your juice, you can know that I will also fumble the whoppers that are sure to come. You are on your own, kid."

Maybe I am reading more into one or both situations than there was—and maybe less. But, regardless, the point is made that *life is problems— just one problem after another.* Life is a Pez® dispenser of problems, whether it is taking time to refill the ice cube tray when there is still one cube in it or leaving it for the next time (person) or whether to steer left or right when a deer runs in front of your car or whether to go to Yale or Harvard or whether to boil the egg 6 minutes or 15 minutes for making egg salad, and so on, ad infinitum. Functional families help their children *prepare* for problems. They use problems as opportunities to teach various problem-solving techniques, decision making, handling emotions, prioritizing, and more.

It's OK to Make Mistakes

Dysfunctional families often lack the ability to solve problems effectively, so naturally, they dread their arrival because the family is just going to get weaker (more tired, more broken, more depressed) each time they pop up. And woe unto the family member who creates the problem by making a mistake. Mistakes are spotlighted and shamed in a misguided attempt to ward off the problem or prevent it from happening again. This is not unlike trying to kill a fly on the wall with a sledgehammer. It might work, but the damage caused is bigger than any benefit that might be reaped. Because there are always going to be mistakes where there are humans, a family where mistakes are not okay is a toxic environment because everyone is constantly trying to blame others for anything that goes wrong. Who wants to be hit with a sledgehammer?

If problems strengthen a functional family, then mistakes are critical to growth of that family. Mistakes are seen as challenges, like a puzzle to be solved. Mistakes are seen as warning signals that we must take action to keep our family safe and healthy, so mistakes help stave off further danger and can easily have a positive spin to them. As a former certified diver who did some salvage work in the Gulf of Mexico, I was grateful for all the mistakes we made in training that gave our instructor an opportunity to remind us that you do not ascend faster than your bubbles or that you always always carry a knife or that you never never dive alone. Our instructor was in the lifesaving business first and foremost. So are functional families.

Riding Easy in the Saddle

A dysfunctional family walks on thin ice. A functional family breaks the ice on purpose—sometimes just because. They can be spontaneous without fear. Functional families laugh. They smile. They can bear down seriously when needed but can just get plain silly, too, because they know that one should not take oneself too seriously all the time in this life because life is to enjoy. Life is not a crucifix. Life is not a jail sentence but, rather, a canvas to paint on, so why not paint it with fun and jubilation, rather than with grayness and antagonism?

Dysfunctional families are so fear-based that they are constantly angry and/or depressed and/or tense, waiting for "the other shoe to drop." They cannot relax. They might buy relaxation tapes, but they get frantic when they can't find them.

Obviously, if a family does not have good problem-solving skills and if the next mistake just might be the proverbial straw that breaks the family's back, how can they be expected to hold the reins loosely? They either become hypervigilant, or out of exhaustion, they escape into something—anything—for relief, whether that might be excessive alcohol or drugs, television, tobacco, daydreaming, sex, shopping, gambling, eating, working, or something destructive.

CHAPTER 10

Life's Toolbox of Skills and Techniques

WITHIN the acorn is everything needed to grow the mighty oak tree, except external nourishment and some protection from the elements, until it is strong enough to withstand hardships on its own. If the seedling isn't nurtured by its environment, it dies or is stunted. This means that the tree may live, but it will have to endure the results of the deprivations suffered as a seedling. This developmental plan is much the same for humans as well, no matter what the culture, ethnicity, or gender of the child.

At conception, we intrinsically possess all the things we need to achieve our full potential as wonderfully enlightened and fully developed beings. Our environmental requirement for these abilities to materialize is to be fully cherished. The supervisors of our environment are called parents. The ideal situation (which almost never happens) requires two very healthy parents to be fully developed as adults, spending most of their time raising the child until it can take care of itself, about two decades in our world today. This implies that the two parents themselves each had two such parents, and they each had two such parents. Unfortunately, the intergenerational legacies of abusive/neglectful child-raising, busy and/or preoccupied lifestyles, and parents' own unfinished business rarely permit such a natural phenomenon to occur.

Utilizing the analogy of a toolbox, the child is born with all the tools necessary to achieve its rightful place in the world. Most of the tools are invisible at the time of birth. Some will acquire visibility naturally through healthy development, while others must be led out by

67

caregivers. Some of the tools deal with emotions, some with communications, and others with interpersonal relationship skills, physical skills, problem-solving and decision-making skills, and so on. The list is very long.

For example, suppose the primary caregiver doesn't know how to handle anger in a productive and healthy fashion. Children learn by example, and if the male child watches the father mishandle anger by pretending it isn't there, until one day he explodes over some seemingly trivial matter, how then would the child know differently except to handle his frustrations in this same "manly" fashion? It really isn't much different from parents not knowing how to use a hammer. For some reason (perhaps there is a belief that hammers are evil in this particular family tree), the children are taught to use a pair of pliers (a "pliers are good" legacy) to drive a nail. Pliers will get the job done but won't be as effective or might hurt your fingers or the object being nailed into, but it does get you by. Sadly enough this is exactly what many people do—get by—and believe that's all they deserve and maybe even feel lucky at that! But getting by is hardly why we exist. We know humankind has the potential to rise above the mere mastery of bodily needs and, indeed, can choose consciously to develop.

Just how does the Shadow Child Syndrome prevent us from making increasingly progressive choices? When a dry sponge is squeezed under water and released, the first molecules of water absorbed go the deepest. When it is squeezed again, those same first-in molecules will be the last to exit. Quite simply, this is why parents are so powerful: *They are there first.* Their messages have more power in our lives because of a simple law of human physics: "Two things cannot occupy the same space at the same time." The first message in (grained) concerning a certain topic has the most weight, healthy or not, productive or not. The message goes in, and there it stays with great resistance (inertia) to change, healthy or not, productive or not. This is because the human mind has one big operating need besides survival: *the need to be right.* It needs to be right about its conclusions, healthy or not, productive or not.

The need to be right is understandably necessary to function and survive. Upon deciding to cross the street, you say to yourself, "It's okay to cross, right?" Without a responding "Right!" from within, you might remain standing indecisively on the corner forever. It is important to feel right about one's perceptions and decisions in order to move ahead with conviction in one's life. But, not unlike many life issues with dysfunctional family survivors, this need can become confused and often inappropriately applied.

Because of ineffective child-raising, our ego becomes warped with this need to be right, even to the point of self-destructive stubbornness, and indeed, many of us humans might be said to stubbornly die prematurely of "terminal righteousness." Normally we get by with justifying our perceptions of the world. We rationalize our shortage of tools and skills in a manner that allows us to be righteous, not only about our discomfort, but also about our unfulfilled destiny as fully potentialized human beings. We grow up honestly believing that life is hard, nice people finish last, and true happiness is probably (hopefully) achieved only after death. We even proclaim with t-shirts and bumper stickers such beliefs as "Life sucks, and then you die." These attitudes are perpetuated by the Shadow Child Syndrome in individuals. Also perpetuated are violence, mental illness, criminality, war, terrorism, continuances of child abuse and neglect, and much physical suffering and illness.

The only way to stop the ignorance and violence against self and others in our families, schools, businesses, and society is to

1. Understand exactly what constitutes abuse and neglect
2. Refuse to perform or enable further harm
3. Be able to accurately assess the appearance of the Shadow Child Syndrome symptoms
4. Institute programs that counteract, not just symptoms, but the underlying causative and perpetuating factors

> Dealing with symptoms is like locking the armory after the weapons are in the streets.
> —Joseph Califano, Former Health, Education, and Welfare Secretary

Abuse, Neglect, and Susceptibility

The core issues to understand are *abuse, neglect,* and *human susceptibility.* Abuse is causing harm (the opposite of protection in the oak tree example), and neglect is lack of nurturing (nourishment in the oak tree example). Humans are particularly susceptible to long-term effects from abuse and neglect because they are very sensitive, extremely intelligent, and highly adaptable.

Human Sensitivity

The component that makes people spiritual, empathic, caring, and capable of being supportive and compassionate has a downside; it also makes them hyper-vulnerable to the psychological after-effects of abuse and neglect. It goes with the territory in that, if one is going to care about others, one is also going to be open to potential injury. Compassion is a two-way street. As an example, in stress psychology research, the major stressors for an individual are created by loved ones and/or relatives. The paradox is that these are the same people (or positions) who can also fill a life with meaning, excitement, and love.

Worst case scenarios of people driven mad by abuse and neglect because of their sensitivity are those who internalize their world of activity, such as catatonics, and those who externalize their world of activity, such as antisocial personality types. Both internalizers and externalizers are reacting against their previous suffering, but in ways that destroy their ability to function in the "normal" world. When they are seen in this context, one realizes one is watching victims in the process of reenactment, or doing unto self or others what was done unto them.

Human Intelligence

Humans are quick on the uptake. They usually don't have to be bitten more than once to get the message. Along with this quick-mindedness is the ability not only to remember events forever, either consciously or subconsciously, but also to let those stored memories accumulate and affect future behavior. We call this ability learning. Children are learning proportionately more the younger they are. In other words, a 1-day-old child is learning more per waking hour than a 5 year old, who is learning more per waking hour than a 15 year old, who is learning more per waking hour than a 25 year old, and so on. Again, one of the very things that makes humans so special has a downside. The swinging door of human intelligence has *Tremendous Potential* written on one side and *Damaged Easily* on the other side.

Worst case scenarios of people driven mad by abuse and neglect because of their intelligence are those who internalize with hallucinations and creative delusions and those who externalize with conniving, manipulating, or rapist mentalities.

> One form of insanity is making the same mistake over and over
> and expecting different results.—Unknown

Human Adaptability

Due in part to our intelligence, humans are incredibly adaptive. We are able to adjust almost instantly to situations in order to get our needs met. This is especially true if we perceive a situation as one that may endanger our survival. This is exactly how abuse and neglect are perceived by the child, that is, as life-threatening. Those in caregiver positions are the keepers of food, shelter, and, most of all, the affection that humans desperately need in order to develop appropriately and healthfully. Abuse and neglect are threats to the supply lines, and children intuitively know which side their bread is buttered on, especially when they are infants.

The sacrifice of the child's integrity with self occurs often and quickly and, at the time, seems a small price to pay to keep the supply lines open. In the long run, however, it can become another form of living death known as codependence. Extreme codependence is the externalized manifestation of someone driven mad to some degree because of haywired adaptability. The internalized form of adaptability gone sour is chronic anger and/or anxiety caused by a constant fear of losing control.

Addiction as Adaptation

Addiction is the inability to say "No" to an event, substance, or person that causes life-damaging consequences physically, mentally, emotionally, spiritually, socially, or financially. Addiction is a prominent adaptation that people manifest internally and act out externally in order to deal with the tear in their soul created by being raised in a dysfunctional environment. At one point in time, it seemed the biggest dysfunctional family survivor manifested disease was alcoholism. Later, it was realized that all chemical dependencies were crutches in dealing with disease and that alcohol was just one form of drug addiction. This *disease* was finally titled codependence and it emerged into public awareness. It was realized that chemical addictions were just ways of dealing with the pain of living with the disease of codependence. In light of current knowledge, a deeper revelation is possible. *This book proposes that the major addiction in this world is the addiction to abuse. Alcoholism, drug addiction, codependence, and others are just vehicles for abusing the self and others.*

Hypothesis: Anyone with a less than nurturing family of origin easily develops a process addiction to some form of abuse, whether as perpetrator, victim, or enabler.

This process addiction is a direct result of abuse/neglect in any form by primary caregivers, which resulted in damage to the child's pristine self-esteem. This means that the child learned to disregard the true self and began to adapt by adopting a false self in order to be more pleasing to caregivers. This self-defeating adaptation is perpetuated through an inner drive to affirm subjective conclusions about reality through internal and external reenactments. The denigrating message that is learned and repeated to the self over and over is, *I am the kind of person who needs and/or deserves abuse and/or neglect.* In order to be correct about this belief, the survivor attracts and creates a self-fulfilling flight plan of abuse and neglect in one or more of its many hydra-headed forms. Judging by the list in Appendix I, there is no shortage of ways in which this prophecy can be self-fulfilled.

Without intervention, the means to abuse self and others physically, emotionally, mentally, or sexually are continually discovered by dysfunctional family survivors. There is also an attraction to affiliating with other "carriers" who become part of the drama. And it *is* a drama. This is not Nature's plan, no matter how frequently it occurs and how normal it appears. We only need to remember Nazism to know that just because millions of people declare certain actions sane does not make them so.

The "natural plan" becomes evident just by watching a human baby born into a secure environment with a low-trauma delivery system. The baby is genuine: WYSIWYG (What You See Is What You Get). It is fully real and pure as an angel. Its skin even smells of sweetness. Its emotional expressions are exactly proportional to its own interpretation of reality, not someone else's that it has become codependent upon. Because of the power of its purity it will activate anyone around it! We are tantalized by the newborn's ability to reflect, not unlike a mirror, our own unfinished family of origin business. If we were abused as an infant, we may feel a need to hurt the child and/or modify its behavior so it won't be so genuine, i.e., make it smile when it doesn't want to, make it stop crying because it bothers us, make it sleep when it apparently wants to be awake, make it eat when it isn't hungry, and so on ad infinitum. The infant has the need to survive like the rest of us and adapts to the tune of reinforcement, real or perceived. Thus it begins to abandon its self, and the pattern of abuse is formed. And, since we all do it, it appears quite normal.

But, of course, any untreated adult survivors around the baby don't really know what normal is—one of the major characteristics of the Shadow Child Syndrome.

The baseline premise behind all received abuse is that, *I am not acceptable as I am.* If I am being abused (a self-validated subjective experience) then I know I am not being cherished at this moment for what and who I am, and I feel mistrustful and ashamed. If this becomes a recurring pattern in my childhood, I develop a core of mistrust and shame. This core, not unlike plutonium rods (energizing, but insulated and hidden) in nuclear reactors, becomes a toxic driving force, motivating destructive behavior inwardly (self-abuse) and/or outwardly (other-abuse). Because of its widespread nature, it can, indeed, become second nature. It infiltrates our families, our schools, our industry, and our institutions. It is highly contagious, enabling it to spread rapidly from person to person and generation to generation. A personality core of mistrust and shame is the fundamental cause of the Shadow Child Syndrome.

> So the one fish swims up to the other fish and says,
> "What do you think of this water today?"
> And the other fish replies, "What water?"

Is it possible that children could feel like a panicked fish out of water without abuse and neglect in their daily lives? If so, would they not then invest abundant energy in keeping it around and inside them?

CHAPTER 11

The Many Forms of Abuse

B REAKING the addictive cycle of abuse begins with awareness. Awareness is not always comfortable. Awareness of abuse is never comfortable. It is, however, necessary to become aware in order to break the vicious cycle. To paraphrase William Blake: "In order to escape from prison, the first thing you must do is realize that you are *in* one."

Toward a Nomenclature of Human Abuse and Neglect

In Appendix I there is a developed numbering system of the various forms of abuse and neglect. Professional educators, school counselors, social workers, and therapists are encouraged to use it in their field and discuss it with clientele and colleagues alike to spread its utility. There are several powerful rationales behind this attempt to classify, a main reason being that it may be the only method that can provide a language that will communicate to people with judicial and legislative power in a way they can both relate and refer to with confidence.

The task was to develop a clarifying nomenclature, or definitive classification system, of abuse and neglect in order to encourage an accurate universal language for utilization by the public and professional sectors alike. This system greatly clarifies communications regarding traumatic incidents in people's lives. The goals accomplished by adopting a nomenclature are:

1. Universal recognition and agreement as to the exact practices that are abusive/neglectful
2. Clear definition of abuse/neglect forms
3. Establishment of a coded classification system for concise denotation and documentation
4. Provision of a foundation for the establishment of an accurate database for assessing the short- and long-term effects, including cost factors, of abuse/neglect on human beings
5. Creation of a set of standards upon which to evaluate the current projected effectiveness of specific behaviors and practices utilized with children
6. Provision of an accurate assessment system by which society's health, education, legal, and human welfare agencies can make critical decisions affecting defenseless children and their futures

With the standards set by the Classification System of Child Abuse and Neglect (CSCAN) in Appendix I, all of us have probably abused others, have allowed others to abuse us, and/or have abused ourselves. We are probably going to continue to do these things. The question is: Do we wish the abuse to increase, stay the same, or decrease in frequency? If we wish it to decrease, we *must* become more aware of all of the forms of abuse, including the subtle ones that we erroneously pass off as "harmless."

Definition of Abuse and Neglect

The CSCAN in Appendix I views abuse as an act of commission and neglect as an act of omission. Despite the context commonly assumed and usually reinforced by the media that inflicting physical harm has more impact than any other form, what is true is that the long-term psychological effects of both abuse and neglect are similar. Abuse is obviously overtly harmful, while neglect is, although covert, still damaging. It can be stated that neglect often creates more harmful effects because it is more difficult to identify and, therefore, is not seen as the toxic agent that it is.

- *Abuse:* an act which is not accidental and harms, or threatens to harm, a person's physical, mental, or emotional health or safety

- *Neglect:* an act of omission which results, or could result, in the deprivation of essential services necessary to maintain the minimum mental, emotional, or physical health of a person

Although not listed as a specific category in CSCAN, all abuse/neglect, no matter what form, is ultimately spiritual abuse because it facilitates the creating of a *false survivor-self.* This essentially manifests *a separation from the genuine self, the main ingredient in the definition of spiritual abuse.* One of the greatest tragedies of abuse and neglect is that survivors wander through life never knowing who they really are. Without intervention, they cannot find their way home to a restored sense of true self.

[It is suggested that the reader now turn to Appendix I to review the CSCAN before proceeding further.]

Section III

The Syndrome of
Shadow Children

CHAPTER 12

The Shadow Child Syndrome

THE Shadow Child Syndrome is a condition that occurs as a direct result of being raised by anyone other than nurturing caregivers. Children develop many of the following eight personality traits in order to survive abusive and/or life-threatening environments. Shadow Children carry these adaptational traits through their growing years and often unnecessarily into adult lives that are limited by these same strategies. More often these traits in adulthood are legitimized in various ways, rather than being seen as pieces of handicapping, unfinished business. Having thus been rationalized, they go unaddressed and are easily perpetuated across and down through many family layers. In other words, this life-strangling insidiousness can become an accepted part of a family's legacy to its children for many generations.

In a subsequent chapter, we will look at these eight characteristics of the Shadow Child Syndrome again in light of the educational environment. Although the eight are ever-present, they manifest themselves differently in different environments. Because of the intensity of schools, symptoms of the syndrome often come out sideways or camouflaged.

Survivor Traits of Shadow Children

Control Consciousness

Growing up in unstable and unpredictable environments creates chaotic inner feelings and uncertainty. One learns to be watchful and cautious in order to survive. One learns to control emotions, thoughts, and behaviors through suppression and denial, hoping that this will help control the self, others, and the world. One feels he/she must have some control in order to have predictability in an unpredictable world.

Avoiding Emotions

The dysfunctional training children receive instills a denial of what was felt: "Don't trust any of your emotions to benefit you, and ignore what your senses tell you." When adults showed emotion, it was often associated with abusive situations, and children assume a direct cause and effect relationship. The message is, "Don't trust others and their emotions, and don't trust your own emotions either."

Inability to Grieve

Especially noteworthy in dysfunctional family survivors is the inability to grieve losses to completion. The "tunnel of grief" has four sequential stations: (1) shock and denial, (2) anger and/or fear/bargaining, (3) sadness, and (4) acceptance and/or gratitude. Inability to grieve means that with each need-to-let-go situation, one gets stuck in one of the stations and never reaches the stage of acceptance. Changes are constant in life. With each change usually comes a death, whether it is leaving the first grade for the second, quitting cigarettes, letting go of one's youth, quitting a relationship, or leaving home. Inability to grieve to completion means that there are many Shadow Children in perpetual states of shock, denial, anger, fear, and/or sadness.

Guilt from Overresponsibility

The guilt carried in the dysfunctional family survivor core stems from feeling overly responsible for caretakers' actions and feelings. The Shadow Child may even feel guilty for the abuse suffered and perhaps for any punishment that siblings received. Shadow Children carry to school and into eventual adulthood the habitual and overwhelming pattern of feeling the need to caretake others. Whether they do it or not is another thing, but if they do not act it out, then they will *act it in*. This means that they will internalize the lack of action as feelings of guilt and inadequacy. Either way, no matter how much caretaking they actually do or don't do, it will never be enough. That is because this is compulsive behavior, and with compulsive behavior: *If what you want is not what you need, it will never be enough.*—Janet Woititz

Crisis Addiction

Inconsistencies, surprises, and perhaps terror were the norm in the childhood of Shadow Children, so when things are calm and stable, Shadow Children may feel deadened or bored, thereby necessitating an urge to stir things up. Although they may complain outwardly about chaos, Shadow Children may be uncomfortable deep inside when it is not present. Some Shadow Children develop an excitement addiction and will generate an uproar game if things are too serene. Often, this appears as sabotage in school, business, or relationships. *They just can't stand success* might be a phrase that sometimes applies to Shadow Children.

Guessing at Normality

What is normal? Since most dysfunctional family survivors' home lives were extremist in nature, no standards were established for the concept of normality. As they grow, Shadow Children are constantly confused as to what is really healthy and normal. They frequently feel unsure inside, although they may have complex strategies to portray themselves as otherwise.

Low Self-Esteem

Being abused and neglected delivers the message, "You are not good enough the way you are." When self-adjusting brings the same response again, one perceives, "The truth is that no matter what I do, I am not good enough." Thus, the core of shame overshadows the pristine self, and Shadow Children regard themselves as defective or irretrievably damaged. It is impossible to develop a benevolent self-concept in this soil. Shadow Children find many ways to reaffirm the belief that they are, indeed, always "less than" in thoughts, words, and actions. It is this self-validating, internalized assumption that delivers the crucifying mandates by which Shadow Children often shape their lives as they try to prove they are right in the less than nourishing beliefs they have formed.

Compulsive Behaviors

One of the earliest evaluative scales we all learned as infants was pain versus pleasure. Human beings avoid pain and seek pleasure. The psychological pain of being alienated from the true self is one of the most intense, confusing, and enduring possible. It resembles an incurable migraine of the soul. Compulsive behavior of any sort offers an irresistible anesthesia for the psychological pain in addition to a pleasant diversion for the body. One can be compulsive about almost anything: alcohol and other drugs, work, gambling, food, shopping, hoarding, sex, exercise, relationships, religion, particular emotion lookalikes (rageaholism, sadaholism, phobias), power, money, violence, and more.

The Shadow Child Syndrome and Limits and Boundaries

If one could locate an underlying theme of the eight characteristics of the Shadow Child Syndrome, it would be about distorted external and internal limits and boundaries. Limits are self-determined lines in the sand of how far I am going to let myself go; "I am only going to eat 2000 calories today." "I am going to quit work at noon today." "I am not going to loan you any more money." Boundaries are self-determinations about how far I am going to let you go; for example, "You cannot talk to me like that." "Don't come over to my house without calling first." "If you hit me, I will call the police." "Don't ask me that anymore."

The simplest definition for a good upbringing is one in which a child learns how to healthfully set limits and boundaries for himself or herself in such a way that he/she prospers physically, mentally, emotionally, socially, and spiritually for the rest of his/her life. Dysfunctional upbringing wreaks havoc with this important ability. As an exercise in this, look back over the eight Shadow Child Syndrome characteristics and interpret them with limits and boundaries in mind.

Recovery

Recovery is the process of working to uncover the natural self so there might be restoration to a balanced way of life. In this way, the Shadow Child (whether still a child or grown up) can enjoy being true to his/her and others' genuine selves. Recovery is often accomplished through 12-step groups, counseling, and support groups, which are all various means of personally resetting limits and boundaries. Sometimes, more concentrated recovery work is necessary, such as therapeutic treatment, rehabilitation, and/or medication, which are all means of having structured limits and boundaries established for the individual. A general rule of thumb is that the more intense the abuse and neglect was, the more intense the recovery work will usually have to be.

[A special acknowledgement goes to my good friend, Dr. Steven Farmer, for his pioneering work in the recovery field and for his assistance in developing the dysfunctional family survivor characteristic list that led to the Shadow Child Syndrome. Steven is a psychotherapist from Laguna Beach, California, and is author of four books, *The Wounded Male, Adult Children of Abusive Parents, Healing Words,* and *Sacred Ceremonies.]*

CHAPTER 13

Implications of the Shadow Child Syndrome in the Educational Environment[7]

CHILDREN bring unfinished business to school in their pencil and lunch boxes, and educators bring their unfinished business in briefcases. At the starting bell they snap open their respective containers and begin throwing the contents on each other. It lasts all day. It wears everyone out and is usually given the general title of discipline problem. Because of misidentification and ignorance, nothing ever gets resolved, things can even be made worse, and everyone usually ends up frustrated, resentful, depressed, and burned out. Usually, the most creative response to all the expanding symptomologies is that the school policy manuals get thicker every year. The first symptom of the Shadow Child Syndrome, *control consciousness*, is ironically never more obvious than in the educational environment.

Control Consciousness

Schools are mostly about control. Can the kids control their urges and learn to delay gratification? Can the teachers control themselves enough so that they will be the kind of educational technicians that can create that magical thing known as the learning environment? Can the

---

[7]This chapter explains implications of the Shadow Child Syndrome for our most popular institution in the United States: education. This chapter is not meant to be all-inclusive, as such an attempt would be voluminous. The purpose here is to quickly give the reader a flavor of how this thing called the Shadow Child Syndrome looks in action and some insights that might show strategic intervention possibilities.

administrators control their images, energy levels, budgets, and staff in order not to look bad yet still carry out the edicts created by the federal government, state legislature, state department of education, local school board, public, parents, business leaders, changing times, and so on?

A trained family systems therapist can walk through a school and, after listening to a few minutes of several conversations and watching the corresponding body language, interpret for you a whole universe of the unfinished family business that lurks behind most interactions in the school. It's mostly about fear—the fear of losing control. Although the therapist's interpretation will be correct, nobody will want to hear it and will either deride or promptly ignore it. This is because the interpretation *is* right on the money, and as the old saying goes, the truth hurts.

Every year, our schools are becoming bigger and bigger catch basins of unfinished family of origin business influencing every person in them. To be honest with you, I personally wouldn't teach in a school today unless the staff were aware of this. Dysfunction is most dangerous when denied, meaning that more dysfunctionality is going to be perpetrated because denial is occurring. This is what we mean by a "highly toxic environment." In their ignorance and denial, some professionals are treating poison victims with bigger doses of poison. And it's all done in a futile effort to heal the pain, or at least control it. One of the goals for researching and publishing these findings is to halt the process of naively trying to put out fires with gasoline.

Control Modalities for Children

It is natural for healthy children to want to learn, grow, and develop. We assume the school environment and its personnel are encouraging this development. But what if the child is blocked from natural progress by dysfunctional control mechanisms learned from a dysfunctional home? How might we identify those modalities in Shadow Children?

Retreat Modality

Passivity, shyness, withdrawing, phobias, anxiousness, fearfulness, and spiritual limpness are various expressions of someone suffering from a general mistrust that the "environment is friendly." For that person, life has perhaps become a series of abusive/neglectful episodes, and the best strategy is to run as far away as possible. It makes sense. It looks odd when the reaction appears although the threat isn't apparent in the school environment, but we must remember that we carry our historical universe with us in our internal microclimate and *that* is where we react from. Think of these Shadow Children as having retreated into the recesses of a cave as far as they can go. It's lonely and damp in there, but it appears safer than what masquerades as life-giving sunlight outside the cave. In what way could you reassure these cave dwellers that they could dare take the risk to come out and try once more to develop? Once you get them out, what would you have to do to sustain that trust? (Also see The Tunnel of Grief section below.)

Aggressive Modality

A good offense is the best defense. Sound familiar? This is a fairly accurate truism in our world today. Its roots are in childhood. Let's be honest, we admire someone who fights back, who stands up after being abused, and growls, "Enough!" Why don't we admire this spunk in kids? Because it's often misplaced. They can't fight their abusers and neglectors. Either they don't know who the abusers are because it was camouflaged or justified, or it's too dangerous to confront the offender. (Did you stand up and growl at your parents when they cracked you one or called you names, or did you take it out on someone else/yourself?) What do these children need? Acknowledgement of their wounds and a chance to heal them, plus training in how to creatively express their pain. They will also desperately need to learn from a healthy model about how to go about setting limits and boundaries for themselves in society. Schools have an excellent opportunity to be this model. Democracy must be reinvented every generation. The general environmental rule in school should be, "We will give you educational opportunities to set your own healthy limits and boundaries, but if you can't we will do it for you until you can. Our goal is to help you learn how to healthfully self-monitor and self-adjust your life toward quality outcomes."

Mental Illness Modality

Few mental patients come from functional homes. Children with mental illness are unconsciously trying (unsuccessfully and unhealthfully) to fill a need. Mental illness is a means of controlling either the external or internal environment to reduce threat or pain. It may show up in the forms of obsessive behaviors, dissociation, depression, self-abuse, violence, chemical abuse, and/or antisocial behaviors. If an educator knows that the root of the aberrant behavior is a lost child trying to cope, then one can more easily endure the search for them in their darkness. Be a friend with a flashlight leading them to either healthier patterns or to someone who can teach them healthier patterns. Know your sources for referral.

Overachieving or Underachieving Modality

Trying to be more than you are is self-abusive, and trying to be less than you are is self-abusive. A healthy life is accepting the self as a developing entity with a potentially great, although unknown, future, and feeling good about that. Kids dramatically over- or undershooting their academic targets are often trying to prove themselves to be somebody they are not and unconsciously using the curriculum as a vehicle of self-abuse. Be suspicious of students who look miserable (anxious, sad, frantic) no matter how much they overachieve and students who look too satisfied with underachieving.

Avoiding Emotions

If children aren't emotions, what are they? If humans aren't emotions, what are we? But children are supposed to "let it out." One comical view of school is to see it as a bunch of little emotional agendas running up against a bunch of totally emotionless curriculum guides, policy manuals, and schedules. In actuality, that is more of a tragedy than a comedy, because it occurs in schools on a daily basis. Shadow Children coming from dysfunctional environments often exhibit a twisted approach to emotions, what they are, and how to express and resolve them appropriately.

Q: What is the school's response to children's emotions?

A: A good day is when children have no emotions and just quietly do their work.

Q: What should the school's response be?

A: Emotions are normal responses—neither good nor bad—to the environment, and they have an onset, sequence, and an end. They are indicators of what we love or fear and, as such, indicate our values. There are healthy ways to experience and benefit from your emotions. Let us accept emotions as a normal part of the day and show students how to effectively handle their emotions as part of the curriculum.

Inability to Grieve

I have listened to adult clients showing little emotion as they offer up a laundry list of abuses heaped upon them as children. When finished, I would ask them what they did not get as children that they wished they would have gotten, and that was when the hurt and tears began to show. Most every one felt ashamed to admit they felt betrayed, ripped off, or denied what we all needed as children: a healthy, loving, safe, and nurturing family that accepts—no, affirms—us exactly as we are. The shame, via an erroneous and misguided sense of sinful selfishness, felt by these adult survivors is what blocks the grief work necessary to finally lay to rest a childhood full of heartbreak.

The Tunnel of Grief

Children in school exhibit their unfinished grief work in a number of ways. If one looks at the "tunnel of grief" needed to fully accept any separation, it facilitates understanding of where children might get stuck.

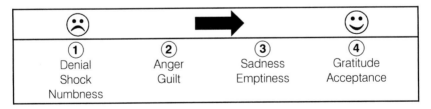

It is helpful if we empathize with children (or anyone) who is suffering a loss. In some ways, it is when we are most human. We can productively learn about the tunnel of grief by utilizing our own experiences. Take a moment and clearly remember a past separation with which you are not comfortable. It could be a death; a loss; a separation from a person, place, or job; phase of life; or behavior. Think about this still painful or unfinished separation for a moment, and then reflect: "In which stage of grief am I still stuck?"

Stage 1. Shock/Denial/Numbness: Are you still numb? Do you say, "I can't bear to think about it"? Do you have difficulty remembering it? Does it seem hazy, faint, or far away? Does your mind have trouble staying focused on that past separation?

Stage 2. Anger/Guilt: Are you resentful? Do you feel cheated or ripped off? Could it be that you really need to feel anger but won't let yourself because it may appear trivial, selfish, silly, or futile? Or do you feel angry at yourself (guilt) for not doing all you feel you should have done?

Stage 3. Sadness/Emptiness: Are you depressed about it? Feel the need to cry about it? Inconsolable? Hurt? Empty? Lost? Lonely? Exhausted?

Stage 4. Gratitude/Acceptance: Do you see how you benefited from the experience, person, or thing from which you are now separated? Do you feel peaceful or pleasant when you remember? Do you have insight about how that experience/person/thing has helped you to cope better with your life today? If so, you have at least made an initial journey all the way through the tunnel of grief.

Know that, if the separation was highly traumatic, you may need to go through the tunnel for the same event more than once in order to peel the internal layers of the tunnel. It is comforting to know that each layer is easier and faster than the previous one. One day, when you have completely "cored out" the tunnel, it will vanish, leaving only nostalgia and gratitude.

There are three helpful things to remember while in the middle of the grieving process: (1) It is natural, healthy, and necessary to grieve the many separations we must pass through in our lifetime; (2) it is helpful to breathe in nice slow circles with a relaxed exhale when experiencing grief (this allows the body to surrender to the truth of your emotions); and (3) know in your heart that this pain is temporary—that it *does* pass, contrary to the feelings that may make it seem endless.

The grief process is about becoming honest and taking responsibility for our emotional lives. Successful grief work liberates us from our past, allows us to ride easy in the saddle of the present, and promotes enthusiasm about our ability to handle whatever the future may bring.

Back to our major point: We may discover kids in various stages of grief at any time. Students who are called airheads or daydreamers or unconscious are probably in the first stage of grief and don't know how to move past it. They are in shock, denial, or just numb from the experiences of abuse/neglect. Angry kids have been denied the love that they need and are feeling ripped off. Sad children are experiencing the void or seemingly endless sea of emptiness. A professional educator can help move children through the stages to gratitude and acceptance so they can get to a proactive state of being naturally in the moment and can begin to rebuild their lives in a manner deserved from the beginning. If an educator feels awkward or insecure in doing this, they should refer the child to a counselor.

Guilt from Overresponsibility

Probably the saddest children to witness are the ones who try to become little adults too soon. Unfortunately, we often mistakenly call these children good because they more than likely become overachievers or even little helpers for the teachers. It is important to look behind the scenes here and make sure that we are not enabling an already unhealthy pattern. Children are not supposed to be developing such broad shoulders when they have such little bones. If this is not discouraged, Shadow Children will grow up into classic enablers themselves.

Guilt is all about breaking rules or standards. The guilt-ridden statement "I am not a good person" means that I have not lived up to the standards of goodness. But just whose standards of goodness have been internalized, and are they clear, healthy and appropriate? Children trying to grow up too fast are often attempting to be surrogate parents or even spouses in the name of "goodness." This easily taints or even kills the precious flower of childhood.

Crisis Addiction

Kamikaze kids: they look like they can't stand success. Just when things are starting to go well, Shadow Children screw it up. (Please note, again, that some Shadow Children act out and others act *in*, but these are just two sides of the same coin. They are *acting a symptom* either way.) If this applies to a child in your life or school environment, then know that this is the symptom being played out. With some Shadow Children, during crisis is the only time they feel electrically alive. With others, although it may look like they just want attention, it is the strategy they have adopted to get a semblance of affection—negative attention being better than none at all, much like bad breath is better than no breath at all. These children need to be shown more appropriate paths to get their needs met. They need positive attention when things are calm or means of getting affection without playing the uproar game.

Guessing at Normality

How could kids coming out of some of the homes they do have even an approximation of what the concept of *normal* means? They have been in a pool of such craziness and abuse/neglect that their standards of normalcy are either warped or nonexistent. They have mostly been trying to survive, not worrying about social standards of acceptance. The school must model sanity and a limits and boundaries system based on an established range of acceptable normalcy. Democracy must be reinvented every generation. Children usually must rely on the school to learn the system of concern for peers built upon the Three Musketeers slogan, "All for one and one for all!" If the school cannot establish this productive counterculture for a child, then all is usually lost for that particular individual. Fair or not, the school is often the last bastion for teaching sane and healthy social interaction. If the school itself is a poor example, then the only safety net left for these children is a life of institutions, prisons, or death (living or otherwise).

Low Self-Esteem

Shadow Children, like everyone else, are born with naturally healthy (some call this high) self-esteem; however, it becomes covered over with environmental pollution in a dysfunctional family. The school's function is to provide a counteracting force where children can prove to themselves that they deserve the self-esteem with which they were born. Unfortunately, out of pure ignorance, the school system often unwittingly revictimizes the victim. Schools, although they should know better by now, still naively expect children to come to school with all their "oars in the water." When the kids don't fit the expectations of the curriculum guides or normed behavioral standards for their grade levels, they are then seen as little cognitive deficits and are either discarded or, with well-intentioned (but still poisonous) tongue-clucking, patronizingly labeled and treated like moronic cattle—none of which serves to uncover the healthy self-esteem needing to be expressed.

Success is the greatest esteem-builder. If an educational system is so deficiency-based (always looking for what is missing rather than what is present) that it is unaware of constantly sending the all too familiar message to the child: "Oh, and another thing wrong with you is, . . ." then it becomes a collaborator in the soul-killing system already established for the child by his/her dysfunctional home environment.

Compulsive Behaviors

For ease of explanation, I want to lump addictive and compulsive behaviors together. Let us just agree that we are discussing children who are into destructive cycles of behaviors or habits that they cannot say "No" to. Again, compulsive-addictive behaviors are actually a form of mental illness, but many of them have become an acceptable norm in large parts of our society. We easily become blind to them because, as classic dysfunctional members of the bigger societal family ourselves, we have developed a high tolerance for inappropriate behavior and pain. But just because we have gotten used to cigarette smoking, alcohol consumption, work addiction, gambling, hypo- and hyper-eating problems, relationship addictions, and more does not take away their destructive impact on society or its Shadow Children.

A healthy school environment, by definition, must establish a confrontive (truth-telling) attitude toward self-destructive behaviors and, if it has the resources, provide support for recovery from such behaviors. Here is where good role-modeling, school support groups, school counselors and psychologists, and satellite services pay off. Compulsive-addictive behavior patterns are tough to break because they give a little shot of pleasure along with a lot of temporary relief from pain (no wonder they are so prevalent!). The countermeasures have to be commensurately healthy and determined enough for a fight that will last the long haul. _Confrontation does work_, as statistics have shown in systems that have targeted specific destructive patterns with hard-hitting programs. Always expect a fight. Nobody wants to give up their placebo because it feels like the only life raft on the ocean to them. The answer is to provide a more attractive raft.

CHAPTER 14

At-Risk Program Considerations

T HERE is no established distinctive success formula for an at-risk program. The formulae vary dramatically across the country. Some programs have failed, and some have succeeded. There has either been enough success with pullout programs for at-risk students or enough desperation and frustration with at-risk students in the traditional classrooms, or both, to encourage a mushrooming of these programs across the country over the last decade. Regardless of the reason, because of this explosive increase in at-risk student programs we are now constantly, almost daily, gaining knowledge about what structures and practices may encourage success and what may not. In the next chapter, we will look at two specific programmatic recommendations under the title of Positive Youth Development and the NAREN Nine Facets of Quality At-Risk Education. Briefly, here, we look at some general considerations.

- *It is not what, but how, that makes the difference.* The subject matter takes a back seat to a nonpunitive, more positive, individualized, and compassionate means by which it is delivered.
- *Small is better.* Smaller student–teacher ratios provide more quality time in which personalization can replace anomie, communication can supplant silence and retreating behaviors, and attitude adjustments become probable. Subject matter and learning methods can be tailored to unique student needs and learning styles.

97

- *Learn as I do, not as I say.* A startling discovery is that most at-risk students are whole-to-part learners—85 percent according to Jerry Conrath. Traditional schools are set up for part-to-whole learning: learn this little piece, then this one, then this one, and one day you will get the "big picture." This is unintelligible, boring, and/or crazy-making for at-risk learners. Research shows that at-risk programs that are experientially and project based succeed well because the bits and pieces that need to be learned fit meaningfully into the big picture; i.e., "Oh, I see a good reason for doing all the work it will take to learn this."

- *I get to choose?* Learning healthy independence includes making choices and enjoying (or suffering) the consequences. In a smaller, more closely supervised environment, failures can become the grist for quickly learning effective choice-making while "the iron is still hot."

- *Tough love.* Pull-out at-risk programs allow the creation of an extraordinary environment—structured differently, but nevertheless *structured* with a lot of positive attention to student capability and success. Accountability and restitution are major concepts in at-risk education.

- *Clear procedures provide clarity.* What is the *mission* of the program, its *goals*? Is it a disciplinary program (a soft jail), or a problem-solving program (therapy)? What are the entrance requirements and exact procedures for getting into the program? What is the structure of both the content and discipline program? How does the program interrelate with the traditional school, the student's family, legal and social services, and the community? All of this and more should be clearly spelled out from the beginning. Of course, a lot of it will be modified later through tailoring and monitoring and adjusting.

- *Charismatic teachers.* It takes a palm tree to teach in an at-risk program successfully. She/he has to know how to flex to the ground while having a spine of bamboo; i.e., the teacher who wishes to teach resiliency must model it. A good rule is the 4F rule: firm, fair, flexible and friendly.

- *Charming environments.* The at-risk school/classroom setting should reflect the personality of the humans inside it. This becomes a living affirmation to students that their very presence makes a noticeable impact. At-risk learning environments may not make the Better Homes and Gardens feature page, but they will make people feel like they *belong.*

- *Learn life skills.* Whole-to-part learners want to learn about work, money, family, and activities, fitting in relevant content areas as needed. Math makes sense when dealing with a real money issue. Writing has meaning when filling out a job application and creating a resume. Honing communication skills is relevant when it immediately creates a happier relationship. There are many models, and the 4R Character-Building Curriculum—respectful, responsible, reflective, resourceful—provides a clear picture of this particular consideration.

The 4R Classroom

Teaching just the 3 R's to our children today will guarantee their failure in tomorrow's world.

Responsible

|

4R

Reflective —   — *Resourceful*

|

Respectful

The 4R curriculum prepares youth with the *character* to live well and succeed in the 21st century. It is boldly progressive and individually tailored to students, thereby providing a ready model for inclusion, the discouraged learner, and other individually needs-based curriculum efforts. It is not a replacement for subject matter, but a concurrent thematic foundation woven into content.

RESOURCEFUL
stamina
content area knowledge
computer skills
problem-solving skills
choice-making skills
conflict resolution skills
money management skills
creativity—esthetics
strong identity → confidence → success cycle

The Warrior

RESPONSIBLE
internal locus of control
healthful interdependency
self-initiating
determination
collaborative skills

The Citizen

RESPECTFUL
nonabusive
compassionate
charitable
concerned
empathic

The Friend

REFLECTIVE
meditational
critical thinking
psychotechnologically savvy
contextual fluidity—multiple realities
insightful
global consciousness

The Philosopher

4R is a K–12 curriculum designed to promote healthy, vibrant, and productive students who will be empowered (have tools and skills) to promote enthusiastic lives for themselves, their families, and society.

Fundamental training in progressive thinking; physical conditioning; and technological, social, and economic skills are the platform of the curriculum. 4R borrows liberally from such new paradigmatic areas in education as multiple intelligences and realities and emotional intelligence.

4R students are prepared in four major character areas: warrior, friend, citizen, and philosopher, representing resourcefulness, respect, responsibility, and reflection. For younger children these are represented by the tiger, wolf, porpoise, and owl. Students are immersed in all four character areas throughout the curriculum, with flexibility for them to major in one or more to suit their needs, goals, and particular personalities. Other character areas can be negotiated.

4R classrooms are envisioned as mentally, socially, emotionally, and physically active classrooms, with an obvious character-building emphasis. Constructivist and project-oriented modes are prevalent, with individual needs-based assessments being continually performed by the teacher. Student assessment is via electronic and tangible portfolios. Lectures by teachers are limited, because most character learning is socially or individually oriented. Prevalent learning strategies might be learning centers, projects, cooperative learning, computer-assisted instruction, internet education, student research, discovery, simulation, and learning packets.

A Tongue-in-Cheek Look at What *Not* to Do!

There are many ways to make a point. In such a serious business, perhaps a more humorous description of considerations is not out of place. In other words, let's lighten up a bit!

Checklist of Considerations for Program Failure
or
How to Increase the Odds of Your At-Risk Program Failing!

- Make sure it's seen and used as a "dumping ground."
- Underfeed (underfund) it.
- Keep the program a secret.

- Dehumanize and sterilize it with lots of imposed policies, rules, and regulations.
- Be vague about the program's purpose and structure.
- Insure the curriculum is irrelevant to the students' real world.
- Overcrowd it.
- Hire drill sergeants and burnouts as teachers.

Checklist of Considerations for Staffing Failure
or
How to Increase Your Odds of Failing by Hiring Educators
with the Worst Possible Characteristics!

- Treat the students as damaged goods.
- Teach the same content in the same way that they had it in the mainstream, i.e., in the identical manner they had trouble with the first time!
- Utilize sarcasm and put-downs.
- Be inconsistent, nervous, flighty, and flakey.
- Embarrass students in front of others as a coercive technique.
- Be inflexible.
- Have no sense of humor.
- Be apathetic, uncaring and insensitive.
- Exhibit a negative disposition with verbal and body language.
- Teach meaningless and unrelated content to the student.

Summary Statement

It is my firm conviction that there is a deep and abiding prejudice against at-risk students. I mean a prejudice that is no different from the prejudice toward African Americans that, in 1954, made *Brown v. Topeka Board of Education* a necessary decision. This prejudice springs from the same contaminated fountain that pays women less than men for the same jobs, calls Asians "gooks," and says certain people, because of their characteristics, do not have the same rights. We look down on children whose parents are on welfare, are in prison, or who immigrated to this country and need special help in our schools. In schools, we do not open our arms unconditionally to all. We do not.

I think it is a psychological problem. It is a problem that will be very difficult to legislate away, because it rests in the psyche of many in our population. The only way to overcome this prejudice is with exposure to others different from us, in order to discover they are not different at all. Perhaps legislation can assist with that—mandating that we must associate with those we would prefer not to. In the final analysis, however, it will be up to each individual to have the humility to admit that he/she was initially prejudiced and that the reason for that prejudice was a myth clung to in ignorance. How many people have what it takes to do so?

Anecdotal stories can be misleading, but this next one has stuck with me so strongly for so many years that I believe it to be an iconic example worthy of relating. In teaching my college psychology classes, I hated just lecturing because it seemed a perfect way to take exciting material about our own humanity and turn it into a train to Snoozeville. To combat this malady that besets many a college class I had, in this instance, I set up a role-playing exercise on decision making wherein students were sorted into groups of six. Each group was playing the part of a hospital board in a small town faced with a terrible dilemma. There was one life-saving machine available and 10 people who needed it within 60 minutes. In other words, nine people were going to die, and one fortunate person was going to live, depending on what the board decided in the next hour. Each role-playing group was given short biographies of each of the 10 potential recipients.

I knew this was a tough assignment. It almost seemed cruel to put people into such a pressure cooker situation. I relished it. No one fell asleep, and discussions were heated and anxious. Some amazing statements were overheard. Some were compassionate, some quite intelligent, and some shocking. One stood out to me more than the others. One of the 10 fake case studies included a young man of 22 who had been a high school dropout and was now working in a lumberyard. I heard 20-year-old Roxie declare in her group, "Well, the dropout is out. He had his chance and blew it!" Some of her classmates paused, but most just crossed his name off their lists without hesitation.

Having been an at-risk kid who considered dropping out and having had friends who had been forced to drop out because of family issues or who were pushed out by a school that would not fit academics to conditions in the kid's life that he could not control, I was horrified at how automatically the word dropout made you a social reject.

Did I mention that all of the students in my class were in the teacher education program?

I was so disturbed by her comment that I asked Roxie to stay after class. I liked her. She was a fireball, a dedicated student with a burning desire to be a great teacher.

I said, "Roxie, I overheard your comment about the dropout quickly going into the ineligible category without further consideration."

She repeated, "Yep. He had his chance and blew it."

"Yes, I heard that too. Perhaps there were extenuating circumstances; maybe he didn't want to drop out, but had to."

"Look, Dr. Jones," she continued, "I studied hard in school—it wasn't easy for me. I have a math phobia and failed it twice here in college, but I got a tutor and passed it. I only got a C, but I passed it, and I never quit. I have little sympathy for kids who quit. They will never amount to anything."

"Who told you that?" I challenged.

"Everybody knows it," she replied, her eyes flashing righteously.

Everybody knows it. Well, maybe they know wrong. But maybe if enough educators know it, they can make it come true so they don't have to appear wrong. We all know teachers often have a thing about being wrong. Enough so that they might subconsciously ensure that the self-fulfilling prophecy be fulfilled? Does society need scapegoats to feel better? Are we so sure that mainstream achievers are worth more to our world than those who don't always fit in?

It is time to look more deeply at the central issue. It is not only the core issue in prejudice, but it is also the issue that will add more certainty for success in an educational program for Shadow Children. It is the issue of *respect.*

If at-risk children are to succeed in school, they must be respected. Once respect goes out the window so does any chance for a fruitful relationship between student and teacher. Why would Shadow Children, already downtrodden in so many ways, invest genuine effort into academics unless they feel their educators care for them, respect them, and are willing and able to provide the support they need to help reclaim themselves?

CHAPTER 15

A Case for Separate At-Risk Education Standards

There is little consistency in applying quality standards to educational programs for at-risk students. Yet, if we take the preceding chapters to heart, it is obvious that we must care for Shadow Children enough to shape the educational environment for an optimal fit to their unique needs. Since its inception on January 1, 2001, NAREN has been attempting to derive from all available research a means by which quality at-risk programs could be instituted systemically and nationwide. This has taken the form of creating a vehicle that directs resources to more effectively stem this tide of discouraged learners. Again, I am the Director of this fine organization, and my drive comes from my deeply felt conviction that NAREN will solve a problem that will reduce pain and open doors of success for many who now suffer and face closed and locked doors.

What follows is a general introduction to the NAREN schema for evaluating at-risk educational programs. It is also a succinct attempt to provide guidance and leadership to establish a foundation for effective design and implementation of a quality program for at-risk education. Assessment is often the Trojan horse of educational reform.

The NAREN Nine Facets of Quality At-Risk Education

NAREN titles its research-based scaffolding Quality Facets of At-Risk Education Programs. It currently comes in the form of a 130-page Self-Study Kit that allows schools to either build new effective programs from scratch, revitalize programs that are not working, evaluate existing programs, or to gain certification of credibility and quality.

There are three major themes residing within each facet of the NAREN Nine:

- *Curriculum-wrapping:* personalizing the curriculum in a holistic manner that acknowledges the value of each student's individuality
- *Authentic assessment:* clear indicators that a student and staff are moving in successful directions
- *Monitoring and adjusting:* humility to admit mistakes, along with subsequent willingness to redirect efforts more productively

The NAREN Nine

The nine facets for quality at-risk programs that NAREN has identified are as follows.

Accelerated Academic Curriculum

Most at-risk students learn differently and not at all slowly when they are engaged appropriate to their learning styles and needs. High expectations that are reasonable and reachable are called for with an integration of academic and work-based learning. *Meaning* is a key component to learning and especially for at-risk learners. Acceleration is accomplished by setting high and clear goals, with meaningful material matched to learning style—signifying that each student has his/her learning individually prescribed.

Strong Literacy Component

"Can't read? Go to jail!" might as well be the banner under which the swelling population is entering our jails and prisons. Next to alcohol and other drug abuse (AODA) issues, illiteracy is the number one qualifier for poverty and/or criminal behavior. The logical and rightful place to stem this tide is in the school. All academic achievement rests solidly on the ability to read and comprehend well. NAREN certification would mean that a program is (1) assessing reading and comprehension upon entry into the program, (2) prescribing appropriate literacy activities, and (3) monitoring and adjusting the literacy curriculum for each student commensurate with individual needs and abilities to ensure success.

Deliberate Self-Management Program

NAREN research reveals that, if an at-risk program is to be effective, it must include a deliberate atmosphere and program of social skills in self-management and responsibility. School personnel must work toward objectives that increase student self-control, school success, attachment and commitment to education, self-efficacy expectations, and belief in a structure (e.g., guidelines or rules). In schools where such a program is well implemented, student conduct improves substantially.

Personalized Curriculum

NAREN research reveals that, if an at-risk curriculum is to be effective, it must shape itself to the student. NAREN strongly encourages deliberate curriculum wrapping as an intervention procedure with a curricular foundation. Each student has different individual needs, problems, and a personal life journey. A personalized curriculum holistically recognizes that one cannot separate academics from personal issues and is structured to deliberately and definitively address issues interfering with achievement and success in all facets of a student's life.

Project Experiential Work Orientation

NAREN research reveals that, if an at-risk curriculum is to be effective, it must offer a whole-to-part curriculum—students fully engaged in a productive enterprise that makes learning relevant to their learning style. A solid work component with major emphasis on developing a positive and productive work ethic is essential to high school–age at-risk students. School-based businesses run by students are highly encouraged. For elementary-level at-risk students, this component is still important but experiences should be age-appropriate, for example, a mock store where students can learn about working in groups, handling money, planning, decision making, prioritizing, problem solving, accountability.

Smaller School and Class Size

Research does not conclusively show a direct correlation between smaller class size and increases in achievement scores. NAREN believes that success is not only about content-centered scores, but also about self-esteem, confidence, and the ability to be productive and healthy. A key factor in this kind of success with at-risk youth is often creation of closer student–teacher and student–student relationships. Smaller classes allow teachers to individually prescribe instruction and monitor progress and encourage more interactivity. Smaller schools foster a sense of family/community, identity building, and caring relationships that enable successful adjustments and transitions.

Solid Planning and Administrative Support System

NAREN research reveals that if an at-risk curriculum is to be effective, it must have a clear mission statement, based on a definitively stated philosophy of education and commensurately cohesive teaching and learning strategies that are research-based and have solid theoretical foundations. A collaborative, communicative, and supportive administration model is highly recommended, with obvious evidence that staff and students are highly prized.

Collaborative Community Model

NAREN research reveals that if an at-risk program is to be effective it must involve collaborative efforts with various educational stakeholders in the community: parents, business leaders, law enforcement and the judicial system, social service agencies, and institutions of religious faith. Evaluations of community involvement programs indicate that these programs can consistently affect positive outcomes for attendance and persistence in school. The effects range from small to substantial but are always positive. Not to be ignored is the positive influence of local higher educational institutions. They are often influential with students prior to high school graduation in numerous ways and set a tone of expectation regarding life-long learning as a viable option for all.

Comprehensive Staff Development Program

Some alternative programs come and go with few lasting benefits for their students, and teachers often become suspicious and reluctant to buy into further "promising" reform efforts. Alternative at-risk models are very complex and often require intensive study, effort, and time to effectively implement. A successful program must include a deliberate and pertinent staff development schema in which teachers are in contact with skilled trainers in a variety of professional development settings at the school and in the classroom. Distance and online learning, in-house interactive involvement with experts, video-conferencing, attendance at conferences and trainings, and professional association membership offer both substantial assistance and support for modern teachers in an educational world, all sitting squarely on a needs-based curriculum.

Conclusion to the NAREN Nine

Certification, standards, guidelines, code points, rubrics—what are they all about? They are concerned with establishing a structure, or scaffolding, that channels resources (time, money, energy, people, materials, etc.) in the most productive of directions. It is always a matter of opinion(s), but research-based opinion is less speculative and has been field-tested under controlled circumstances in an attempt to sort out the variables that truly make a substantial difference toward improving the chances of success for at-risk youth.

Positive Youth Development

With permission from the American Psychological Association (APA), I have taken the liberty to distill an additional and potentially powerful proactive assessment model from an excellently researched APA article by Richard F. Catalano et al., *Positive Youth Development in the United States: Research Findings on Evaluations of Positive Youth Development Programs.* Catalano et al. (2002) not only delineate, but also clearly define 15 characteristics of effective programming for youth:

1. Promotes bonding
2. Fosters resilience
3. Promotes social competence
4. Promotes emotional competence
5. Promotes cognitive competence
6. Promotes behavioral competence
7. Promotes moral competence
8. Fosters self-determination
9. Fosters spirituality
10. Fosters self-efficacy
11. Fosters clear and positive identity
12. Fosters belief in the future
13. Provides recognition for positive behavior
14. Provides opportunities for prosocial involvement
15. Fosters prosocial norms

Positive Youth Development Characteristics Defined

- *Bonding program facet:* One or more of the program's components focuses on developing the child's emotional attachment and commitment to a healthy adult, positive peers, school, community, or culture.
- *Resilience program facet:* Program emphasizes healthy strategies for adaptive coping responses to change and stress and promotes psychological flexibility and a capacity toward successful outcomes.
- *Social competence program facet:* Program provides training in developmentally appropriate interpersonal skills that help youth integrate feelings, thinking, and actions in order to achieve specific social and interpersonal goals and rehearsal strategies for practicing these skills. These skills included communication, assertiveness, refusal and resistance, conflict resolution, and interpersonal negotiation strategies for use with peers and adults.
- *Emotional competence program facet:* Program develops the skills of youth for identifying feelings in self or others, skills for managing emotional reactions or impulses or skills for building

the youth's self-management strategies, empathy, self-soothing, or frustration tolerance.

- *Cognitive competence program facet:* Program seeks to influence a child's cognitive abilities, processes, or outcomes, including academic performance, logical and analytic thinking, problem solving, decision making, planning, goal setting, and self-talk skills.
- *Behavioral competence program facet:* Program teaches skills and provides reinforcement for effective behavior choices and action patterns, including nonverbal and verbal strategies.
- *Moral competence program facet:* Program seeks to promote empathy, respect for cultural or societal rules and standards, a sense of right and wrong, or a sense of moral or social justice.
- *Self-determination program facet:* Program seeks to increase youths' capacity for empowerment, autonomy, independent thinking, or self-advocacy or their ability to live and grow by self-determined internal standards and values (may or may not include group values).
- *Spirituality program facet:* Program promotes the development of beliefs in a higher power, internal reflection, or meditation or supports youth in exploring a spiritual belief system or sense of spiritual identity, meaning, or practice.
- *Self-efficacy program facet:* Program includes personal goal setting, coping, and mastery skills or techniques to change self-defeating cognitions and negative self-efficacy expectancies (the perception that one can achieve desired goals through one's own action).
- *Clear and positive identity program facet:* Program seeks to develop healthy identity formation and achievement in youth, including positive identification with a social or cultural subgroup that supports their healthy development of sense of self.
- *Belief in the future program facet:* Program seeks to influence a child's belief in his or her future potential, goals, options, choices, or long-range hopes and plans or promotes youth's optimism about a healthy and productive adult life.
- *Recognition for positive behavior program facet:* Program creates response systems for rewarding, recognizing, or reinforcing children's prosocial behaviors.
- *Opportunities for prosocial involvement program facet:* Program

offers activities and events in which youths can actively participate, make a positive contribution, and experience positive social exchanges.

- *Fostering social norms program facet:* Program employs strategies for encouraging youths to develop clear and explicit standards for behavior that minimize health risks and support prosocial involvement.

Conclusion to Positive Youth Development

With some expertise and effort, the 15 characteristics of Positive Youth Development could be productively modified into an effective assessment instrument for at-risk education programs. Much like the NAREN Nine, each of the characteristics above could be converted into a Standard statement, along with a sublist of Indicators for each standard, some of which are alluded to in the description of each characteristic listed above. Those Indicators would then be broken out into Benchmarks and Rubrics for accurate rating of program components.

The important point being made here is that there is more than one way to assess an at-risk program. It is not important which one is utilized, as long as it is research-based and field-tested. What is critical is that a quality coherent framework is utilized in order to guarantee excellence in educational programming for at-risk youth.

Assessment instruments are more than just a way to evaluate how we/they are doing. They are creative and formative as well.

Q: "How do we build a great at-risk educational program?"

A: Start with the instrument by which you are going to eventually assess it and build accordingly.

Q: "Our program is off the ground, but wobbly. How can we fix it?"

A: Get the current pulse and profile of what is going on now with the (eventual) assessment instrument and map out a plan for modifying the direction of the program accordingly.

Again, no child asked to be placed at risk. No Shadow Child knows how to fix their problem(s). They rely on us to help them help themselves, and they deserve, just like anyone else in the school system, to be exposed to the best educational programming possible. These are not throwaway human beings; they are children—children looking to adults to show them the way to utilize their intellect effectively to benefit themselves, others, and our society.

Providing quality programming for Shadow Children is a way of saying (1) we are professionals who care, (2) you are in the right hands, and (3) you are not alone in your struggle.

NAREN urges educational systems to rapidly adopt a unique and realistic set of at-risk education standards to open doorways into at-risk educational reform so that all students have an opportunity to attain success.

Section IV

Prevention and Intervention:
Where It Should All Begin . . .

CHAPTER 16

Prevention and Intervention

Factors Influencing Prevention/Intervention Programming

Should schools be involved in prevention/intervention programs? Let us first look at the population demographics affecting today's youth.

As stated previously, the 21st-century family has evolved drastically and has a distinctively different impact on its children (Weissberg et al., 2003):

- Divorce rates are now at 50 percent.
- Unmarried women commonly bear and rear children.
- Dual career parents are the norm.
- Only 30 percent of families have a biological parent working at home and the other in a career outside the home.

Although family configurations have significantly changed and family dysfunction has also significantly increased over the last 50 years, schools have not changed commensurately. Drastic changes in the makeup of modern family constellations and the statistically significant increase in abuse and neglect of children, call for the school to morph itself into a posture where it is anticipating and meeting the curve of change, rather than being constantly behind it.

Q: What is the general mental health of children today?

A: The Surgeon General's Report of 1999 indicates that one of every five children experiences symptoms of a mental disorder during the course of any one year; however, 75–80 percent of these children fail to receive appropriate services (and most still come to school untreated) (U.S. Department of Health and Human Services, 1999).

Q: What is the level of risk behaviors in today's youth?

A: Not good.

- 30 percent of 14- to 17-year-olds engage in multiple high-risk behaviors in any one year.
- Another 35% are considered medium risk being involved with one or two problem behaviors.
- 35 percent have little or no involvement with problem behaviors but still require strong consistent support to avoid becoming involved (Dryfoos, 1997).

Q: What can we truthfully say about the coping skills of today's youth?

A: Relatively low percentages of young people have personal competencies, values, attitudes, and environmental supports that protect against high-risk behavior and encourage the growth of positive behaviors (Benson et al., 1998).

So, the answer to the big question:

Q: Should schools be involved in prevention/intervention programs?

A: It appears that schools are the natural and perhaps only logical choice to launch a widespread, intelligent, organized, and consistent intervention program.

Q: What are the objects of prevention/intervention?

A: NAREN suggests the following hit list of targeted negative outcomes for prevention/intervention strategies when dealing with Shadow Children:

- physical illness
- mental/emotional disorders
- violence
- school failure
- health-damaging risk behaviors

- poverty
- criminal behaviors
- ignorance

Q: What differentiates prevention from intervention?

A: Prevention = actions taken to decrease the number of new cases or incidences of a negative outcome. Intervention = Actions taken to lower the prevalence of existing cases or incidences of a negative outcome.

Prevention

There are four basic approaches to prevention:

1. *Promotion prevention* is not driven by emphasis on illness or social disease, but by focusing on the enhancement of *well-being*. Promotion is utilized to build competence and self-esteem and to increase the quality of life in a general or specific population.
2. *Universal prevention* targets the general public or a whole population group that has not been identified on the basis of individual risk.
3. *Selective prevention* targets individuals or population subgroups that have been identified as possessing biological, psychological, or social factors that place them at higher than average likelihood of being placed at-risk.
4. *Indicated prevention* focuses on high-risk individuals with detectable symptoms or biological, psychological, or social markers that place them at higher than average likelihood of not succeeding in life if intervention does not take place. It is this group that, based on local indicators, is often selected for alternative programs.

Intervention

It is acknowledged that there are many interpretations of the intervention concept, varying across theoretical constructs, value structures, target populations, methodologies, timing, and preferred outcomes, but there are eight proven systemic characteristics of successful at-risk intervention programs for Shadow Children.

1. *Clearly defined target population:* Recipients of an intervention should be clearly identified. As a graphic example, if one could obtain a group photograph of all community members, the target population should be easily identified with an "X" over each member that is to directly benefit from the intervention. This takes time, thought, and discussion.

2. *Clearly defined precipitating behaviors:* The goal of intervention is to halt or reduce negative outcomes. The behaviors that lead to those outcomes are not always clear. Does television lead to more aggression? Does the lack of a recreation center create gang formation? Can afterschool programs reduce teen drug use? It takes time and diligent research to answer these questions.

3. *Comprehensive program approach:* Research into existing successful programs shows over and over again that because human beings are multifaceted, so must effective programs be. Collaboration among the school staff and between the school, the family, social agencies, law enforcement, local businesses, and religious institutions, are needed if the new safety net is to be strong. This means reaching out over time.

4. *Clearly defined program goals:* Goals need to be defined with crystal clear objectives and measurable outcomes. Does a 50 percent reduction in underage drinking mean success or failure? If the dropout rate is reduced by three students a year, is that enough to crow about, or does that mean the program has failed? This calls for thought, discussion, and agreement.

5. *Clearly defined indicators/timelines:* Perhaps there is too much emphasis on final outcomes of programs, and equal attention needs to be given to processes, ongoing practices, climate, and social and emotional aspects. How can one tell if a program is succeeding along the way without waiting for the end results?

6. *Appropriately funded:* If you cannot see the budget, don't start the program. Projected costs need to be thoughtfully determined and backed with serious commitment. It is certainly counterproductive–and almost cruel–to begin a program dedicated to betterment and raise hopes only to dash them (again) because the financial resources were inadequate.

7. *Stakeholder ownership:* It is one thing to get others involved. It is yet another to foster ownership in all parties. The old expression "In

for a penny, in for a pound" is relevant. All partners in the collaborative endeavor should have something to gain OR lose by their involvement. Communication is the key. (Don't forget that the main recipient of the intervention—the at-risk child—must also buy in!)

8. *Persistence:* Persistence always wins, and half-hearted efforts rarely do when it comes to intervention. All stakeholders must be in it for the long haul—not excited if it takes years to see results, but pleasantly surprised if it doesn't. It can take as long to solve a problem as it did to create it. Educational leadership dedicated to a role of constant and long-term support will play a large part in any formula for success.

Selecting for Intervention

I travel the country speaking at conferences and, working with schools and have talked to educators in every quadrant of the United States and in Canada and Mexico. I am a graduate professor of night courses for teachers who are in the classroom teaching at-risk students all day long. Over the years, I have listened to hundreds of teachers and administrators, discussing at-risk education programs, practices, and issues with them. Over and over, some common pieces regarding intervention issues rise to the top of the concern list. They often come in the form of quandaries:

- Why do they wait until high school to start trying to help these kids? It's too late then.
- We know kids are at-risk, but there is no funding/time/personnel.
- There are so many at-risk kids in our schools that we don't know where to start.
- The issues impacting today's youth are beyond the scope of the teacher or school to do anything about.
- There are so many personal issues in kids that, if we deal with those, we cannot teach content sufficiently to do well on the standardized tests we are being measured against.
- There seems to be no way to identify these kids in advance of trouble, so we wind up being policemen and social workers rather than teachers.

Many of these "quandaries" are caused, or certainly exacerbated, by difficulty with identification and timing.

Candidates for Intervention

If you attend conferences and conventions in the genre of at-risk education, alternative education, charter schools, or dropout prevention, you will notice that almost all attendees are working at the secondary level in education. That is the legacy created by a phrase that we have lived with for so long: "at-risk of dropping out of school."

Originally, the at-risk phrase meant being behind in a certain number of Carnegie units to the point where you would not be able to graduate and therefore were in danger of dropping out. The concept of the Carnegie unit was developed in 1906 as a measure of the amount of time a student studied a subject. For example, a total of 120 hours in one subject—meeting four or five times a week for 40 to 60 minutes, for 36 to 40 weeks each year—earns the student one "unit" of high school credit. Fourteen units were deemed to constitute the minimum amount of preparation that may be interpreted as four years of academic or high school preparation (Carnegie Foundation: www.CarnegieFoundation. org).

Why do we wait until high school to identify at-risk students? Tradition? It cannot be because we do not know how to identify these students earlier. Ask any teacher who has been in K–3 instruction with children for a few years and they will tell you without a doubt that they can identify potential dropouts long before even middle school! Many teachers at the aforementioned at-risk education conferences have been heard to say, "Why aren't there more elementary and middle school teachers here?" because they know that education has the ability to intervene much earlier than after children have sat through literally years of school being "behind"—some just waiting until they can drop out.

Utilizing input from literally hundreds of elementary and middle school teachers over a 5-year period, I assembled and field-tested a simple instrument both to make teachers aware of the issues children are facing and to provide leverage for taking action with an effective intervention program.

Selecting for Intervention at the Elementary School Level

Early Assessment of At-Risk Behaviors (EAARB) is a preliminary assessment for classroom teachers to determine if pre-school/primary children are probable for being at-risk of not succeeding (see Figure 16.1).

Figure 16.1. E.A.A.R.B.—Early Assessment of At-Risk
Behaviors in Children

E.A.A.R.B.
Early Assessment of At-Risk Behaviors in Children

Date completed:_____by_____

Check each one that applies for:_____
                                          (child's name)

___ *Direct evidence of neglect
___ *Established evidence of abuse
___ *Sustained sadness and/or monitored for depression
___ *Known family history of abuse, neglect
___ *No one home when child arrives from school/left alone for long periods
     of time
___ *Poor school/academic performance
___ *Not reading by 3rd grade

PHYSICAL HEALTH:
___ Shots not complete, waived
___ Continual health problems
___ Comes to school hungry
___ Doesn't get good night's sleep/falls asleep in class
___ Low birth weight

HOME:
___ Lack of parent support
___ Hopeless, e.g., "My dad won't sign this."
___ Parent/family does not value education/schools
___ Pulled out for vacations or activities with no regard for time missed
___ Missing 10 or more days in 1st semester
___ Two (or more) households, e.g., "Where do I go tonight?"
___ Little or no structure at home

(continued)

PERSONAL:
___ Does not have many life experiences
___ Wants to be loved by anyone
___ Bargains for friendship
___ Gives up easily/needs excessive teacher support
___ Emotionally immature for age in the classroom
___ Poor attitude toward school; doesn't care
___ Seeks teacher attention negatively
___ Disconcerted/flustered (almost lucky he/she got to school at all)
___ Angry
___ Lack of organizational skills
___ Lack of self-confidence

Scoring:

[Name of Child]_____

Circle appropriate category below.

Green - Warning:
Checking 1 *ed item
or
Checking 2 or 3 non-*ed symptoms

Orange - Danger:
Checking 2 non-*ed items
or
Checking 1 * item and 2 or more non-starred items

Red Zone - Critical
Checking 3 or more *ed items
or
Checking 2* items and 3 or more non-* items

INTERPRETATION GUIDE

GREEN - WARNING – School personnel should be on alert and exhibit
deliberate heightened awareness in watching for an increase in existing
signs, or the addition of new ones. Weekly re-assessments with EAARB by a
designated responsible professional are now warranted.

ORANGE - DANGER – School personnel should initiate a responsible and
deliberate intervention to halt further damage to the child and to begin a
specific recovery program.

RED ZONE - CRITICAL – School personnel should initiate a referral to the
proper authority outside the school and begin an immediate collaborative
effort with that/those agency(ies) in a strong intervention effort on behalf of
the child.

Selecting for Intervention at the Middle School Level

Assessment of At-Risk Behaviors in Middle School (AARBMS) is a preliminary assessment to be used by teachers in determining if middle-level youth are probable for being at-risk of not succeeding (see Figure 16.2).

Both the Early Assessment of At-Risk Behaviors in Children and the Assessment of At-Risk Behaviors in Middle School are also available in licensed forms (which are life-time licenses with free upgrades) from www.AtRiskEducation.Net under "Books and Materials.

Figure 16.2. A.A.R.B.M.S.—Assessment of At-Risk Behaviors in Middle School Behaviors in Children

---

A.A.R.B.M.S.
Assessment of At-Risk Behaviors in Middle School

Date completed:_____by_____

Check each one that applies for:_____
(name)

___ *Direct evidence of neglect
___ *Established evidence of abuse
___ *Sustained sadness and/or monitored for depression
___ *Known family history of abuse, neglect
___ *No one home when child arrives from school/left alone for long periods
of time
___ *Poor school/academic performance
___ *Two years or more below grade level in reading
___ *Has been in possession of drugs, tobacco, weapons

PHYSICAL HEALTH:
___ Shots not complete, waived
___ Continual health problems
___ Doesn't get good night's sleep
___ Delayed physical development/growth (possibly from malnutrition)

HOME:
___ Lack of parent support
___ Hopeless
___ Parent/family does not value education/schools
___ Pulled out for vacations or activities with no regard for time missed

---

(continued)

HOME *(continued)*:
___ Missing 10 or more days in 1st semester
___ Unpredictable home base, e.g., "Where do I go tonight?"
___ Little or no structure at home (lack of positive consistent discipline)
___ Does no work outside of school (homework)

PERSONAL:
___ Does not have many life experiences
___ Wants to be loved by anyone
___ Bargains for friendship
___ Gives up easily/needs teacher support
___ Emotionally immature for age in the classroom
___ Poor attitude toward school; doesn't care
___ Seeks teacher attention negatively
___ Disconcerted/flustered (almost lucky he/she got to school at all)
___ Angry
___ Lack of organizational skills
___ Lack of self-confidence
___ Oversensitive to issues of fairness/injustice
___ Blames others habitually (external locus of control)
___ Cannot follow organizational system (lacks structure, realistic direction/focus)
___ Dirty/unkempt
___ Bullying behavior
___ Does not get along with others
___ Lack of self-confidence

Scoring:

[Name of Child]_____
Circle appropriate category below.

Green - Warning:
Checking 1 *ed item
or
Checking 2 or 3 non-*ed symptoms

Orange - Danger:
Checking 2 *ed items
or
Checking 1 * item and 2 or more non-starred items

Red Zone - Critical
Checking 3 or more *ed items
or
Checking 2* items and 3 or more non-* items

(continued)

INTERPRETATION GUIDE

GREEN - WARNING – School personnel should be on alert and exhibit deliberate heightened awareness in watching for an increase in existing signs, or the addition of new ones. Monthly re-assessments with AARBMS by a designated responsible professional are now warranted.

ORANGE - DANGER – School personnel should initiate a responsible and deliberate intervention to halt further damage to the child and to begin a specific recovery program.

RED ZONE - CRITICAL – School personnel should initiate a referral to the proper authority outside the school and begin an immediate collaborative effort with that/those agency(ies) in a strong intervention effort on behalf of the child.

CHAPTER 17

Preparing Teachers for the War

At-Risk Education Field of Study

IS there a need for a concentrated field of study called At-Risk Education? Eight higher education institutions think so.

The U.S. Department of Education estimates that over 30 percent of today's youth are at risk of dropping out, so they certainly see the problem. Nine colleges and universities must think so. They have recognized the need for and the belief in the teacher preparation institution as having a strategic and opportune position for effective school staff training aimed at both at-risk prevention and intervention programming. Listed below are some of the programs and their particular approaches to at-risk education. These programs are currently active in preparing teachers to prepare at-risk kids, including Marian College in Fond du Lac, Wisconsin, which had the first accredited Master's degree program in at-risk education in the United States. The program descriptions are provided by the institutions themselves.

Marian College, Fond du Lac, WI
Students At-Risk Strand

The Students At-Risk strand will prepare educators to more effectively meet the needs of at-risk students in the classroom. Graduate students will design and conduct an action research project that will aid them in reaching the at-risk student. Students will also be encouraged to become at-risk coordinators and teachers in their schools and continue their effort to meet the needs of at-risk students.

Contact information:
Bob Bohnsack
bbohnsak@mariancollege.edu
Marian College
45 S. National Avenue
Fond du Lac, WI 54935
Tel: (800) 2-Marian
http://www.mariancollege.edu

Gonzaga University, Spokane, WA
At-Risk Concentration Description

The Master of Arts in Teaching, with concentration in Teaching At-Risk Students, meets the needs of today's teachers who face multi-problematic issues in the classroom. The dynamics in the modern classroom are intensified by individual issues of each child. Family violence and child abuse, attention difficulties, emotional problems, and learning disabilities can greatly interfere with the student's academic and interpersonal performance. Teachers struggle with significant challenges for which they often have limited training and few resources. The Master of Arts in Teaching: Teaching At-Risk Students provides tools that teachers need to reach their students. The courses in the concentration are based on research in the field of resiliency and asset development, offering a strength-based approach to student intervention.

Contact information:
aruff@soe.gonzaga.edu
Counselor Education
Gonzaga University
Spokane, WA 99258-0025
Tel: (509) 323-3501

Harvard University, Cambridge, MA
Risk and Prevention Program

The Risk and Prevention (R&P) Program surveys both the causes and the prevention of psychological, academic, social, and health problems among children, particularly as they pertain to schooling and education. The program considers problems—found in both individuals and institutions—within the cultural contexts in which they occur, with an emphasis on developmental perspectives and issues of diversity. Students completing the program in R&P can expect to pursue positions as specialists in prevention and lifelong enhancement programs in both traditional and nontraditional (e.g., comprehensive and full-service) schools, early childhood and youth services agencies, and other educational settings. Graduates work as service providers or program planners and evaluators in public and private agencies focusing on prevention and early intervention for children and youth placed at risk, or they go on to doctoral programs in education, human development, clinical or counseling psychology, public health, social policy, or related fields. A select number of students may wish to continue for a second year in the program to obtain a Certificate of Advanced Study.

Contact information:
gseadmissions@harvard.edu
Harvard Graduate School of Education
Admissions, 111 Longfellow Hall
Cambridge, MA 02138
Tel: (617) 495-3414

University of West Florida, Pensacola, FL
Alternative Educator Training Program

Public educators and case managers are faced with increasing numbers of K–12 students who are classified at risk in regard to probable school failure. Both national and state public education data indicate that the percentage of K–12 students classified as academically at risk for school failure has dramatically increased over the last three decades. In the 1960s, fewer than 20 percent of all K–12 public school-age children and youth were classified by the U.S. Department of Education as at risk of school failure. However, by 1990, that estimate had increased to over 30 percent and continues to rise. Teachers and case managers who have traditional educational training are finding it difficult to cope with or to reach and teach students who are disruptive. While this is not an initial teacher certification program, the Alternative Educator Training Program (AETP) fulfills the State of Florida's need by providing specialized training to work in an alternative education setting. In many cases, the courses in this program may be used to obtain additional certification or for certification renewal.

Contact information:
Dr. John P. Kalashian, Program Coordinator
University of West Florida
College of Professional Studies
Division of Teacher Education
11000 University Parkway
Pensacola, FL 32514
http://cops.uwf.edu/copsweb/teached/alted.cfm
Tel: (850) 474-3158

Park University, Parkville, MO
Master of Education (At Risk)

A nine-credit program dealing with issues that face at-risk students and teachers every day, such as classroom management, characteristics of at-risk students, violent behavior, reading diagnosis and remediation, and more.

Contact information:
Betty Deck
bettyd@mail.park.edu
8700 NW River Park Drive
Parkville, MO 64152
Tel: (816) 584-6335
Fax: (816) 741-4371
http/www.park.edu/ME/atrisk.asp

College of Santa Fe, Santa Fe, NM
5-Year BA/MA with Focus on At-Risk Youth

America's classrooms are changing. Population growth and increased cultural, ethnic, and class diversity demand that teachers understand a broad spectrum of ideas, both about the subjects they teach and the needs of different types of students. No two children are the same, and research indicates that tailoring teaching to fit multiple learning styles inspires curiosity in students, the key to their future potential as learners. At CSF, we teach the theory of multiple intelligences: are you a visual thinker? Maybe you learn best through concepts in music or math. Do you work better in a group setting, or do you prefer to work alone? Professors explain and model these concepts in class, and you, in turn, take your experience to your own classroom. As early as freshman year, you will find yourself observing in local schools and interacting with working teachers and their students. All future teachers are trained in classroom management, which means you will be prepared to take on the varied responsibilities of being an educator as soon as you graduate.

Contact information:
College of Santa Fe
1600 Michael's Drive
Santa Fe, NM 87505
Tel: (800) 456-2673
Fax: (505) 473-6011
http://www.csf.edu/pr/viewbook/edu.htm
http://www.csf.edu/pr/viewbook/edu degree programs.htm

Lock Haven University of Pennsylvania, Lock Haven, PA
Alternative Education Studies Program

The Alternative Education Studies program makes it possible for education professionals to engage in reflective practice while improving teaching and program development skills. The program encourages exploration of methods, research, and epistemologies that focus on both the learner and systemic changes that will benefit all students. The Master of Education in Alternative Education is designed to support professionals in education and related fields. Students will develop skills, knowledge, and competencies that will benefit them in their work in alternative and/or regular education settings.

M.Ed. in Alternative Education—Lock Haven University offers a Master's degree in Alternative Education. The nation's first online program in alternative education offers innovative curriculum, including a series of required and elective courses.

Contact information:
Nathaniel S. Hosley, Alternative Education Coordinator
Alternative Education Studies
Lock Haven University of Pennsylvania
Annex Building
Lock Haven, PA 17745
Tel: (570) 893-6247
Fax: (570) 893-6248
http://www.alted.lhup.edu

George Mason University, Fairfax, VA
Advanced Studies in Teaching and Learning

The 12-credit Education Core component of the Master's degree provides students with learning experiences and activities that simulate requirements for certification by the National Board for Professional Teaching Standards (NBPTS).

The Alternative Education Emphasis is an 18-credit component of the Master's degree, allowing students to specialize in Alternative Education.

Contact information:
George Mason University
Graduate School of Education
Advanced Studies in Teaching and Learning
4400 University Drive
Fairfax, VA 22030-4444
Dr. Joan Isenberg, Director
jisenber@gmu.edu
Tel: (703) 993-2037
http://gse.gmu.edu/programs/astl/pdf/altedEmpForm.pdf

Dr. Rebecca Fox, Assistant Director
rfox@gmu.edu
Tel: (703) 993-4123
ASTL Information:
nfarley@gmu.edu
Tel: (703) 993-3640
http://gse.gmu.edu/programs/aslt

Higher Education and Shadow Children

What should be included in a program that prepares teachers to deal more effectively with at-risk students? It would behoove teacher training and staff development to prepare all teachers *as if* they will be at-risk educators because, simply stated, they *will be* at some point. We need to wake up in teacher training institutions and begin to seriously utilize research-based findings in developing courses to best equip *all* teachers, whether undergraduate, graduate, or in-serviced models, for this eventuality.

What else is being done? In Appendix II there are over 35 organizations, programs, and agencies that *are* doing something! Please become familiar with those pertinent to you and your clientele.

CHAPTER 18

Conclusion

A Concluding Statement for an Ongoing Problem

THE danger in summarizing the complex issue of Shadow Children may cause this major problem to appear less significant than it really is. It is a problem with political, as well as economic, considerations and economic repercussions. It is a problem that demands a faster response in reacting to social considerations from the educational system—a system that responds sometimes much like the Titanic would have if you tried to change its course by pelting it with snowballs.

But no matter what considerations and complexities are raised, it will always come down to, "What next?"

- "What next" is the educational system going to do to join the fight to turn human suffering into human success?
- "What next" systemic changes should we make to improve our offerings to Shadow Children?
- "What next" effective programs *and* practices are we going to implement to compensate for those children coming to school with "shallow tool and skill boxes?"
- "What next" can we do to overcome the prejudice toward Shadow Children so that we remove the subconscious blockages and make the necessary adjustments?

We don't have all the answers. But we do have *some* answers. I will get to those, but first, if we are realistic we have to be willing to self-examine, to ask the question, "Have we met the enemy and the enemy is *us*?" Because if we have answers, yet the at-risk population is still growing, we need to turn over every rock. One rock: Is it possible we aren't changing our practices because we are in our own way of the reform we so desperately need? So permit me to potentially embarrass myself and the educational establishment in a moment of direct honesty.

The Question: Just why might we not be bringing all resources we can to bear on the issue of Shadow Children in our schools? Six possible answers follow.

(1) *Perhaps we didn't know it was that big of a problem.* A former elementary and middle school teacher, who for over a decade has been the education correspondent for a major national media presence, was alarmed when he was apprised of the at-risk statistics in this book. "I had no idea this problem was so extensive!" He is a person in the know, a concerned, well-educated man who tries to keep up with all that is going on in education in the United States. He did not know.

This is one reason this book calls at-risk youth Shadow Children. Much like the shadow economy of the United States (taxes evaded, production and trade of illicit narcotics, bartered goods, household production and unregulated micro-enterprise) has *huge* implications for the nation's Gross National Product—but who knows how extensive and how much its impact is? Therefore, how many people talk about this issue or desire to do anything about it? We are all ignorant about the full impact of a Shadow Children population until we become informed.

(2) *Perhaps we just don't know what to do even if we realize the scope of the problem.* I visit a lot of schools. I teach a lot of teachers of at-risk students. I watch and I listen, and what I hear and what I see are a lot of reasons why we *can't* implement necessary changes: money shortages, staff indifference, school board members more concerned with getting revenge than making a positive difference for kids, administrative politics, and more. But I run into just a few teachers and administrators who state that they not only see avenues of implementation, but they are also *doing something* to make that difference. As long as there are *some*, there is good reason to hope. These few are our role models, our mentors, and our guiding light.

Also in Appendix II, there are dozens of programs that work on behalf of at-risk youth. These are tried and true organizations, not just whimsical or hopeful ideas. So, from now on, it will not be for lack of helping organizations that we forestall action.

(3) *Perhaps we do not know how to design or structure prevention and intervention efforts to stem this tide of failure and suffering in our young people.* Mentioned in this book are two scaffoldings including the NAREN Self-Study Kit and Positive Youth Development guidelines, that basically tell you what to do in order to establish a meaningful and effective program for Shadow Children. Yes, it takes systemic and sustained planning and effort to make a dent, but the architectural plans are in existence to guide the direction of that effort, thereby eliminating a lot of wasted resources and frustration. (Without it being a sales pitch, I should also tell you that there are over 130 currently active *programs* that *are* working with Shadow Children, and there is a descriptive list of over 35 classroom *practices* that *are* working for individual teachers dealing with all the symptoms of the Shadow Child Syndrome on a daily basis. These are available in a password-protected database for members only. Admission to all this information is worth the membership cost alone. Go to www.AtRiskEducation.Net and look under Membership.

(4) *Perhaps we don't care (feel) enough to know enough.* As a former psychotherapist and owner of a counseling office, we dealt with some tough cases of people repeating behaviors despite their destructive and apparent consequences. Some of these people were sent by a judge: "Therapy or jail, take your pick!" Some came because a relative said they either get help or the relationship was over: "I see you drunk one more time and the kids and I are gone!" Some came because their boss made them: "Get help or get another job!" Rarely in our office did we see anyone overcome their habits because of warnings or threats. Occasionally, I would get quite blunt with people who had many excuses why they either had no problem, had no good reason to quit, or relapsed more often than not. I would simply say, "You are not hurting enough yet. The pity is that not only might you take yourself down permanently while bottoming out, but you will more than likely take your associates and loved ones with you. For your and their sakes, I hope you find your least endurable pain soon. Come back when you do. Meanwhile, see ya!"

This *threshold factor* is indeed a mystery. There was a railroad crossing near my home in Ohio back in the 1960s that just had the old wooden X as a warning. Seven people eventually were killed there by trains—one by one over the years. After the seventh death, they finally put up red flashing warning lights at that crossing. I ask myself even today: Why seven? I mean, why after the second death didn't someone say, "Hey, human life is precious. If it had been my wife or child or husband or parent dying on that crossing, in retrospect, I certainly would have found it worthwhile to spend the county tax dollars on a warning light prior to that night!" Why not after three? Why not after four, five, six? No, it looks like *in that case* it took seven deaths. Seven people needlessly wiped out and seven sets of families and friends suffering seemed to be enough to tip the county cash drawer into proactivity about that crossing light. Yet, in the same state, one guy died of an overdose of drinking Everclear (a 190 proof alcohol beverage), and the state outlawed it almost instantly. I guess the magic number of Everclear deaths is one. In the Chicago area Tylenol scare of 1982, seven people mysteriously and randomly died within a few days of each other from cyanide-laced pills placed in retail containers by a murderous individual(s). Now *everything* we buy is tamper-proof. One incident again creates massive change. Yet we have people dying right and left from lung cancer and still allow cigarettes to be sold. People dying in drunken-related highway slaughter (over 42,000 a year in the United States and increasing yearly) is not enough to deter the 120,000,000 drivers who annually self-report driving under the influence of alcohol, according to the National Highway Traffic Safety Administration, nor has it created the legislation necessary to *stop* alcohol-related deaths. (If only the number seven would work in that category!)

Another angle on this not caring enough to know enough was brought to light by the President of the United States in 2000 when, on camera live, he stated, "And I approve of alternative schools," and then in an aside comment to someone, "You know, those are schools for children who cannot learn." Every at-risk educator must have cringed like a tortoise when they heard that! Obviously, even the leader of the most powerful nation on the globe doesn't know enough for some reason. I have wondered how many people overheard his statement and thought, "Yeah, let's just stop wasting money on those kids!" If you care enough to know enough, you find out that all humans are capable and love to learn *under the right circumstances.*

(5) *Maybe we didn't know just how expensive it was NOT to do anything.* One purpose of this book is to make that statement clearly, as shown in Chapter 2. It costs almost as much not to address the Shadow Child problem as it would to *annually* rebuild and secure five Afghanistans and five Iraqs, according to The Every Child Matters Educational Fund. They also point out in their findings:

- For every $1 invested in afterschool programs, $3 come back through reduced juvenile crime and improved school performance.
- For every $1 invested in quality pre-kindergarten programs that improve school readiness, society gets $7 in benefits.

So, now we know that "the pay me now, or pay me a *whole lot more* later" concept is driven home. There is only one reason remaining that I can think of, and I risk offending you to mention it. Please do not take offense. I believe we all are prejudiced in some ways, so it is not an indictment to be so. More important is to find the truth and be set free. If it stings a little, the liberation is worth it—much like a pneumonia shot is much better than the pneumonia!

(6) *Perhaps we are prejudiced against Shadow Children!* Once we have removed all the overt reasons for not being more systematically and financially dedicated to supporting our Shadow Children, what is left except this uncomfortable psychological conclusion? We love to exhibit our forefinger and thumb at right angles to one another on our forehead and exclaim, "Loser!" We only want to see winners. No one remembers who came in second in the Boston Marathon or the NBA standings or who lost the World Series in 1980. We love to watch the bad news on the evening news so we can feel superior and say, "Wow, I am not like them!"

If the President thinks at-risk kids cannot learn, if the general populace thinks of Shadow Children as an inconvenience, if we can only lament on how much money it costs us for special programs and teachers to remediate, if we look down our noses at the less fortunate, if we blame these children for the circumstances they did not create, if we wish they would all just go away, we need to do two things:

1. Wake up our intellect and learn enough to care enough. To that

end, this book and the Bibliography provide a great deal of information.

2. Wake up our empathic feelings to experience what it must feel like to have two strikes against you and then to go into a school that sighs and/or sneers at you as if you were a lower caste member. These children need reassurance, hope and enlightened programs and personnel from the profession.

Many think inaccurately that prejudice is based on not knowing enough about your object of prejudice. In actuality, prejudice is thinking you know enough when you don't. You overcome prejudice by getting close to and familiar with your object of prejudice, rather than distancing yourself.

I ask my students, "How do you learn to like the most dislikable of your students?" Then I answer for them:

Look into their eyes, see the real child and invite them to come out,
Look past symptoms, speak to the causes, hurts, fears, and self-doubt,
Do not get caught up in the obvious exterior view,
For underneath that child's surface is someone just like you.

Here is something that can be done, makes everyone feel good, doesn't cost a cent, and probably prevents dropouts!

The Secret Angel Club

A dear friend of mine, Steve Hartley, tells of the results of a study he did in 2002 with Shadow Children who dropped out in Madison, Wisconsin. Almost every single interviewed dropout felt that no one in authority ever noticed them; they never felt connected to the school, and this was one of their major reasons for leaving school.

This is preventable. Some things may not be. Some things may be difficult to overcome. That Shadow Children are not noticed is a black eye made blacker by the fact that it is preventable and we do nothing about it. But we can. Here's how.

- Elect a Secret Angel Club coordinator
- Secretly identify Shadow Children in the school
- Recruit Secret Angel Club members—any adult in the school can

be an angel if they are willing to commit 10 minutes a week to change a child's life. Sometimes custodial people make the best angels!

- Pair a secret angel with at least one child. Don't overload your angel. Note: A designated child cannot be in an angel teacher's classroom.
- Once a week, the secret angel should make eye contact with the child and say something positive and/or smile. Suggestions are:

"Well, hi there, Susie!" (With a look of pleasant discovery)
"Oh, Bob, you look super today!"
"Hey, Linda, how's it going?"
"Well, doesn't Chantall look terrific today?!"
"There you are, Harold! I was wondering if I would see you today!"

- It's the direct eye contact and welcoming body language that makes the difference. Sometimes a big smile and a hand wave will do, particularly if it is awkward to use words in certain surroundings.
- Make a point of "finding" the child in different places of the school.
- Spice it up and think of ways you can make a kid's day special in subtle ways.
- Avoid giving gifts of any kind—just your caring attitude is enough. Don't share with anyone (besides other Secret Angels) who your child is by name.

Classifying Abuse and Neglect

Why Is Abuse Harmful?

THIS question may appear silly to ask, but not when you consider how prevalent abuse is, and has been, down through time. Millions have justified abuse, often righteously. Just think of the many clichés: "The best defense is a good offense" (and, of course, I have the right to defend myself!); "Spare the rod and spoil the child" (and nobody will like the child if it's spoiled so I'm doing it a favor!); "This hurts me worse than it does you" (it's your good fortune that you have someone willing to suffer in order to teach you such a valuable lesson!); "We must have order" (and there just is no better way to achieve this order than to punish you!). If you have read the abuse list in Appendix I, then you realize that there is practically no end to abuse. We are, like the fish, immersed in it to such a degree that we no longer notice it. Despite all the laws, commandments, morals, ethics, and poetry pleading down through the years, we still have a plethora of abuse occurring on a nearly constant basis. It seems almost legitimate to say, "Come on, let's be honest; abuse is a way of life—we just have all these little 'rules' to keep it under control. Just don't get caught and it's no big deal. Don't be so naive."

Indeed, just what is so bad about abuse? Answer: It goes against the "Plan"—the plan of actualizing our human destiny, of achieving a natural state of lightness, sensitivity, beauty, health, and intelligent concern for self and others.

It is proposed by some that the ultimate human-body purpose is to reach a state of consistent spirituality. If that is true or is at least supposed to be true, it is very difficult to acquire this blissful harmonious state and participate in abusive behaviors at the same time. It is simply a law of physics that two things cannot occupy the same space at the same time. Abuse and spirituality cannot occupy the same human at the same time, or better stated, one cannot express one's positive spiritual nature while being abusive. It is also very difficult to express one's spirituality while allowing oneself to be abused.

Abuse is incongruent with human destiny. That is the reason abuse is painful.

> "Don't ever forget, Miss Radha: To the senseless, nothing is more maddening than sense. Pala is a small island completely surrounded by twenty-nine hundred million mental cases. In the country of the insane the integrated man doesn't become King." Mr. Bahu's face was positively twinkling with Voltairean glee. "He gets lynched!" [Island, Huxley, 1962, p. 78]

Remember: Just because history seems to verify that abuse is habitual doesn't make it sane or humane.

So, abuse is destructive because: One can never be deeply, satisfyingly, healthfully, harmoniously, and genuinely human in the midst of abuse.

Most people, it seems, want a wholesome, peaceful lifestyle more than anything. They started out as innocent, genuine, loving, spontaneous humans as babies and then lost these positive characteristics because of abuse. They can get them back by saying "No" to abuse in any form, by recovering from abusive patterns that have been internalized as coping mechanisms, and by learning all they can about this accepted destructive philosophy of nihilism.

Relationships of Abuse Forms

The potential negative consequence of all abuse/neglect is a rupture in the victim's relationship with his/her pristine self. This creates a dynamic in which all forms of abuse/neglect can ultimately result in spiritual abuse—damaging the primary and foundational relationship with self. This explains why sexual abuse often creates the deepest damage in the individual.

Sexual abuse interferes directly with our identity, because primarily we identify ourselves by our gender. The first thing everyone wants to know when a newborn arrives is its gender. This is so that "it" can be related to as an individual identity. The very foundation of personality formation rests upon gender in our society. Sexual abuse casts shame and doubt upon the manner by which the victim relates with his/her own core personality orientation. This can have pervasive and long-term damaging consequences for the victim in all his/her future relationships.

Likewise, emotional abuse is very powerful because emotions are both physical and mental and provide the psychosomatic link between mind and body. Thus, emotional abuse is two-pronged and affects all parts of the victim's world.

Classification System of Child Abuse and Neglect

The overall benefit of a nomenclature, such as the Classification System of Child Abuse and Neglect (CSCAN) below may be that it provides, for the first time, substantiated evidence of the potential impact of specific child-raising behaviors. It answers the question, "How are Shadow Children created?" CSCAN also provides a clear and organized means for communication and documentation about abuse and neglect.

Note: It is important to remember that, psychologically speaking, abuse and neglect are *subjectively validated* experiences. Any legal proceedings for affixing culpability are utilized only to objectify what the victim has known since the moment of violation.

The compilation that makes up CSCAN was originally proposed in the book *Resolving Unfinished Business: Assessing the Effects of Being Raised in a Dysfunctional Environment* and has since been validated and modified through utilization by numerous school systems over the years.

So-called verbal abuse is not included as a separate category in CSCAN because, technically, words are tools or methods of conveyance of other forms of abuse. Words are often used to create mental and emotional abuse. Yelling "Fire!" in a crowded restaurant would be a verbal vehicle for physical abuse. Sexual abuse can also be verbally transmitted; e.g., one can denigrate a person sexually by ridiculing his or her genitalia.

CLASSIFICATION SYSTEM OF CHILD ABUSE AND NEGLECT (CSCAN)

PHYSICAL ABUSE (PA)PHYSICAL ABUSE (PA)

PA.___

01. Deliberate attempted murder
02. Slapping with the hand (not spanking)
03. Shaking with rapid movement
04. Scratching with the fingers
05. Pinching with the fingers
06. Squeezing painfully
07. Hitting with the fist
08. Spanking
09. Pulling hair
10. Beating with objects (boards, sticks, belts, kitchen utensils, yardsticks, electric cords, shovels, fanbelts, hoses, etc.)
11. Throwing
12. Shoving
13. Slamming against walls or objects
14. Utilizing temperature extremes:
    a. burning
    b. scalding
    c. freezing
15. Forcing of food
16. Forcing of water
17. Forcing of objects into orifices (does not include sexual abuse)
18. Utilizing objects to pinch, poke, or scratch
19. Painful tickling
20. Overworking

PHYSICAL NEGLECT (PN)PHYSICAL NEGLECT (PN)

PN.___

01. Attempted murder via willful preoccupation (allowing a person

to enter a life-threatening situation with the intent he/she will be fatally injured)

02. Lack of essentials:
    a. food
    b. water
    c. clothing
    d. shelter
03. Leaving the child alone in age-inappropriate ways
04. Leaving a child who is too young in charge of others
05. Failure to provide medical care
06. Allowing or encouraging the use of alcohol and/or other drugs
07. Failure to protect the child from the abuse of others
08. Failure to protect the child from the abuse of the spouse

EMOTIONAL ABUSE (EA)

EA.___

01. Double binds (a deliberately perpetrated predicament where all choices given the child are negative ones)
02. Projection and transfer of adult problems onto the child (scapegoating)
03. Alterations of child's reality (lying) (e.g.,"Dad's not drunk; he's just tired.")
04. Overprotecting (does not healthfully allow child to experience consequences of its own actions)
05. Enmeshment, or smothering with apparent affection (living through the child)
06. Preventing the child from learning appropriate developmental tasks (trust, autonomy, initiative, industry, etc.)
07. Double messages [e.g., "Of course, I love you, dear" (said as Mom tenses up and grimaces); "I love you just as you are; you just need to change a couple of traits."; "I love spending time with you, I just have to run right now"; and so on].
08. Not acknowledging that abuse or neglect has taken place
09. Using child for personal gain (e.g., financial profit, holding on to a spouse, providing a sense of meaning for the parent, etc.)

EMOTIONAL NEGLECT (EN)

EN.____

01. Desertion or abandonment
02. Failure to nurture, care for, or love the child
03. Failure to provide structure or set limits
04. Not listening to, hearing, or believing the child
05. Expecting the child to provide unreasonable emotional nurturing to adults instead of receiving it
06. Deliberately withdrawing or withholding love
07. Caregivers not being emotionally present because of:
    a. mental illness
    b. chemical dependency
    c. depression
    d. compulsivity in themselves
    e. compulsivity in the family environment
    f. extended physical illness
08. Excessive guilting (dwelling on mistakes)
09. Excessive shaming (characterizing the child as flawed, defective, a "mistake," or at fault for existing)
10. Sarcasm (sideways anger)
11. Inflicting unreasonable fear
12. Minimizing the child's emotions ("You shouldn't feel sad, angry, afraid, happy, etc.")

MENTAL ABUSE (MA)

MA____

01. Excessive blaming (overloaded with criticism)
02. Degrading
03. Name calling
04. Put-downs by comparisons
05. Excessive teasing
06. Making fun of, laughing at, belittling
07. Nagging or haranguing

08. Screaming
09. Verbal assault (frequent "jackhammer" barrages of words)
10. Manipulating, deceiving, tricking (deliberate misleading)
11. Betraying
12. Cruelty
13. Intimidating, threatening, bullying
14. Controlling or overpowering
15. Not taking child's thoughts seriously
16. Put-downs via patronizing
17. Discrediting (not giving credit where it is due)
18. Disapproving of child's individuality
19. Making light of or minimizing wants, needs
20. Raising hopes falsely, breaking promises
21. Responding inconsistently or arbitrarily
22. Making vague demands
23. Saying "If only you were [better or different]."
24. Denigrated because of gender, ethnic, religious, or racial differences

MENTAL NEGLECT (MN)

MN.___

01. Lack of communication skills development
02. Lack of praise or encouragement to develop intellectually
03. Undereducation
04. Lack of affirmation regarding uniqueness

SEXUAL ABUSE (SA)

SA.___

01. Forced rape
02. Fondling, inappropriate touching
03. Sexual harassment, innuendoes, jokes, comments
04. Leering

05. Exposing self to
06. Masturbating in front of
07. Mutual masturbation
08. Oral sex
09. Anal sex
10. Intercourse
11. Penetration with fingers
12. Penetration with objects
13. Stripping/exposing
14. Sexual punishments
15. Inappropriate or excessive enemas
16. Pornography: taking inappropriate pictures and/or forcing the child to watch
17. Coercing children to have sex with each other
18. Forced sexual activity with animals
19. Inappropriate invasion of bathroom/bedroom privacy

SEXUAL NEGLECT (SN)

SN.___

01. Failure to educate children concerning healthy sexual limits and boundaries
02. Failure to educate children concerning menstruation, conception, pregnancy, birth control, sexually transmitted diseases, and so on.
03. Failure to help children differentiate intimacy issues from sexual issues
04. Failure to help children develop positive self-esteem regarding their sexual selves

VICARIOUS ABUSE (VA)

VA.___

Vicarious abuse is a special case of abuse, in which the victim is part of a family or other system in which someone else is abused in some way. The witnessing of abuse (PA, EA, MA, SA) can be just as damaging as being the actual recipient of the abuse.

You may acquire the latest version of the CSCAN assessment form as a reproducible master copy for your school's assessment needs and a written statement of a right to use from:

NAREN
107½ State Street, Suite 5
Madison, WI 53703
NAREN Web Address: www.AtRiskEducation.net

Please send $29.95 + $3 s/h *per school*. Please include the name(s) and address(es) of the school(s) where the form will be utilized. This is for our records so that we can imprint the specific school name and address on each master copy. Purchase orders are welcome.

Resources

36 Organizations Doing Something!

ARTS PROGRAMS FOR AT-RISK YOUTH

Art programs designed for at-risk youth decrease involvement in delinquent behavior, increase academic achievement and improve youth's attitudes about themselves and their future. Much information can be found at the below web address.

Americans for the Arts
1000 Vermont Avenue NW
12th Floor
Washington DC 20005
(202) 371-2830
(202) 371-0424 (fax)
http://www.artsusa.org/education/youth.html

NATIONAL DROPOUT PREVENTION CENTER

The mission of the National Dropout Prevention Center/Network is to serve as a research center and resource network for practitioners, researchers, and policymakers to reshape school and community environments to meet the needs of youth in at-risk situations so these students receive the quality education and services necessary to succeed academically and graduate from high school.

National Dropout Prevention Center
Clemson University
209 Martin Street
Clemson, SC 29631-1555
(864) 656-2599
ndpc@clemson.edu
http://www.dropoutprevention.org

National Criminal Justice Reference Service (NCJRS)

NCJRS is a federally funded resource offering justice and substance abuse information to support research, policy, and program development worldwide. They offer a prolific database of information on critical issues in at-risk education: crime, gangs, AODA issues, juvenile prostitution, violence, STDs, victimization, bullying, runaways, and more.

National Criminal Justice Reference Service (NCJRS)
P.O. Box 6000
Rockville, MD 20849-6000
(800) 851-3420
(301) 519-5500
(301) 519-5212 (fax)
TTY Service for the Hearing Impaired (toll free): 1-877-712-9279
(local): (301) 947-8374
http://virlib.ncjrs.org

National At-Risk Education Network (NAREN)

The National At-Risk Education Network (NAREN) is a private, nonsectarian, nonprofit educational agency dedicated both to promoting the success of at-risk youth in our schools and supporting the educators who work on their behalf. NAREN is an organization for educators but offers website information for all. Professional associates gain access to a prolific database of proven successful at-risk programs, publications, conferences and a quarterly e-Journal.

NAREN
107$\frac{1}{2}$ State Street, Suite 5
Madison, WI 53703

(920) 907-8337
info@naren.info
http://www.AtRiskEducation.net

National School Safety Center (NSSC)

The National School Safety Center serves as an advocate for safe, secure, and peaceful schools worldwide and as a catalyst for the prevention of school crime and violence. NSSC provides school communities and their school safety partners with quality information, resources, consultation, and training services. The NSSC identifies and promotes strategies, promising practices and programs that support safe schools for all students as part of the total academic mission.

National School Safety Center
141 Duesenberg Drive, Suite 11
Westlake Village, CA 91362
(805) 373-9977
info@nssc1.org
http://www.nssc1.org

National Clearinghouse for Alcohol and Drug Information (NCADI) Substance Abuse and Mental Health Services Administration (SAMHSA)

SAMHSA's National Clearinghouse for Alcohol and Drug Information (NCADI) is the nation's one-stop resource for information about substance abuse prevention and addiction treatment.

They staff both English- and Spanish-speaking information specialists who are skilled at recommending appropriate publications, posters, and videocassettes; conducting customized searches; providing grant and funding information; and referring people to appropriate organizations. They are available 24 hours a day, 7 days a week.

(800) 729-6686
http://ncadi.samhsa.gov

ART START

In the spring of 1991, a handful of artists got together to make art with homeless kids in New York City. Over the next 10 years Art Start became an award-winning, nationally recognized model for using the arts to save lives.

Art Start
285 S. Broadway, Suite 620
New York, NY 10013
(212) 966-7807
(212) 966-8539 (fax)
http://www.art-start.org

National Runaway Switchboard

Every day, between 1.3 and 2.8 million runaway and homeless youth live on the streets of America. One out of every seven children will run away before the age of 18. Prevention takes the combined efforts of everyone who comes in contact with youth. Since 1994, the National Runaway Prevention Curriculum has been available to schools across the country.

National Runaway Switchboard
3080 N. Lincoln Avenue
Chicago, IL 60657
(800) 621-4000
http://www.nrscrisisline.org

National Youth Employment Coalition

The National Youth Employment Coalition envisions a nation in which every young person is assured the full range of educational, developmental, vocational, economic, and social opportunities, supports, and services s/he may need to become a productive and self-sufficient worker, taxpayer, parent, and citizen.

National Youth Employment Coalition
1836 Jefferson Place, NW
Washington, DC 20036
(202) 659-1064
(202) 659-0399 (fax)
nyec@nyec.org
http://www.nyec.org

YMCA National Safe Place

Project Safe Place provides access to immediate help and supportive resources for all young people in crisis through a network of sites sustained by qualified agencies, trained volunteers, and businesses.

YMCA National Safe Place
2411 Bowman Avenue
Louisville, KY 40217
(502) 635-3660
(888) 290-7233 (toll free)
(502) 635-3678 (fax)
nationalsafeplace@ymcalouisville.org
http://www.iglou.com/safeplace

Teen Paths

Teen Paths seeks to help families who are troubled with difficult teens, lacking family unity, failing in communication, and are perhaps wondering how they got in this situation. They endeavor to advocate only well-documented, time-proven programs to help reevaluate, restructure, and unify the family system of rules, values, focus, and communication.

http://www.teenpaths.org

The Usual Suspects

The Usual Suspects Theater Company is a 501(c)(3) organization of professional artists. They bring theater arts to youth, ages 12–21, from foster care and juvenile justice systems. Their programs are designed to cultivate pride, racial tolerance, and social consciousness.

The Unsual Suspects
10536 Culver Blvd, Suite 3
Culver City, CA 92032
(310) 558-3190
(310) 558-3191 (fax)
http://www.theunusualsuspects.org

WeHelpTeens.com

The American Academy of Child and Adolescent Psychiatrists estimates that 7 to 12 million children and adolescents at any given time in the United States are affected by developmental, behavioral, and mental disorders. This site is designed to assist parents with a challenging or out-of-control 12 to 18- year-old.

We Help Teens.com
1350 East Flamingo Road #32
Las Vegas, NV 89119
(888) 669-3839
http://www.wehelpteens.com

The Bureau for At-Risk Youth

The Bureau for At-Risk Youth is an educational publishing and media company whose mission is to provide children, students, parents, adults and professionals with timely and effective tools that help them or their clients make critical life choices. Guidance materials and other publications, products, and resources are offered over the Internet at the company's many websites and through specialized direct mail catalogs. The company offers over 5000 proprietary publications and other products, many of them national and international award winners, including multimedia programs, videos, curricula, information handouts, therapeutic games, prevention-awareness items, and more.

The Bureau for At-Risk Youth
135 Dupont Street
P.O. Box 9120
Plainview, NY 11803-9120
http://www.at-risk.com

StandUp for Kids

StandUp For Kids is a 501(c)(3) not-for-profit organization founded in 1990 to help rescue homeless and at-risk youth. With national headquarters in San Diego, California, StandUp for Kids is run almost entirely by volunteers and has established more than 30 outreach programs in 15 states. The mission of StandUp For Kids is to help homeless and street kids. This mission is carried out by a national volunteer force whose on-the-streets outreach efforts will find, stabilize, and assist homeless and street kids in their efforts to improve their lives. The organization's mission is also furthered through deterrence and resource programs provided in schools and via the Internet.

StandUp For Kids
1510 Front Street Suite 100
San Diego, CA 92101
(800) 365-4KID
(888) 453-1647 (fax)
www.standupforkids.org

Drug Rehab

Drug Rehab is dedicated to the treatment of drug addictions. They provide information and treatment resources for individuals suffering all addictions. Referrals to treatment centers are offered at no charge as a community service.

Drug Rehabs
13223 Ventura Boulevard, Suite E
Studio City, CA 91604
(866) 762-3712
info@drug-rehabs.com
http://www.drug-rehabs.com

North Central Regional Education Labatory (NCREL)

NCREL is a wholly owned subsidiary of Learning Point Associates. As a member of the Regional Educational Laboratory Newtork, NCREL is dedicated to providing high-quality, research-based resources to educators and policymakers in the states of Illinois, Indiana, Iowa, Michigan, Minnesota, Ohio, and Wisconsin.

http://www.ncrel.org

True Life Interactive

True Life Interactive is an in-depth life skills, career development, and motivational training program for youth. It is entirely web-based and helps youth across the United States. True Life guides young people, from middle school through college, to learn how choices made today will create their future. They discover the gaps between their expectations and the real world. By learning how to close those gaps, they create a detailed plan to achieve the future they want.

(866) 471-4285
http://truelifeinteractive.com/index.htm

Eckerd Youth Alternatives (EYA)

EYA is a private, not-for-profit organization nationally recognized for its programs to help youth. Programs serve boys and girls ages 8–18 who are at risk for or exhibit emotional and behavioral problems at home, at school, and in the community. A pioneer in therapeutic treatment in outdoor settings EYA also provides specialized residential treatment and community-based programs for juvenile offenders, and early intervention and prevention curriculum for grade schools.

Eckerd Youth Alternatives
100 N. Starcrest Drive
P.O. Box 7450
Clearwater, FL 33758-7450
(727) 461-2990
(800) 554-HELP
(727) 442-5911 (fax)
http://www.eckerd.org

ARISE Foundation

ARISE Foundation in Miami has been working with troubled teenagers for 18 years. It is their mission to teach children life skills to help them handle the daily stresses that come their way. ARISE has identified 260 life skills and published them in over 100 books and booklets and has created seven-hour training workshops for teachers and staff at schools and juvenile detention centers. In Florida, almost 3-million hours of these evidence-based lessons have been taught to date. Whether it is anger management, self-esteem enhancement, or how to cope with bullies, kids can learn to cope.

ARISE
4001 Edmund F. Benson Boulevard
Miami, FL 33178
(888) 680-6100
(888) 599-3750 (fax)
http://www.ariselife-skills.org

Youth Crime Watch

With programs in 42 states and 11 countries throughout the world, Youth Crime Watch demonstrates that young people can make the difference in keeping their schools and communities safe from crime, drugs, and violence.

Youth Crime Watch of America
9200 South Dadeland Boulevard, Suite 417
Miami FL 33156
(305) 670-2409
(305) 670-3805 (fax)
http://www.ycwa.org

The National Center for Juvenile Justice

The National Center for Juvenile Justice is a private, nonprofit organization. Since its inception in 1973, the Center has been a resource for independent and original research on topics related directly and indirectly to the field of juvenile justice. Although the Center is the research division of the National Council of Juvenile and Family Court Judges, it has its own budget and is responsible for generating its own operating funds.

National Center for Juvenile Justice
3700 South Water Street, Suite 200
Pittsburgh, PA 15203
(412) 227-6950
(412) 227-6955 (fax)
http://ncjj.org

The Lionheart Foundation

A primary objective of the Foundation's Power Source Program is to give juvenile offenders and high-risk and troubled youth effective ways to (1) acquire basic emotional literacy skills—the absence of which have played a pivotal role in their emotional, academic, and social problems and the presence of which serve as positive anchors in the present and into adulthood; (2) constructively manage and heal the anger, grief, shame, rage, and other highly charged emotions that often precipitate negative and high-risk behavior; and (3) help youth develop a healthier, more cohesive sense of self and a positive future orientation.

The Lionheart Foundation
P.O. Box 194, Back Bay
Boston, MA 02117
(781) 444-6667
(781) 444-6855 (fax)
http://www.lionheart.org

National Association for Community Mediation

Community Mediation offers constructive processes for resolving differences and conflicts between individuals, groups, and organizations. It is an alternative to avoidance, destructive confrontation, prolonged litigation, or violence. It gives people in conflict an opportunity to take responsibility for the resolution of their dispute and control of the outcome. Community mediation is designed to preserve individual interests while strengthening relationships and building connections between people and groups and to create processes that make communities work for all of us.

National Association for Community Mediation
1527 New Hampshire Avenue NW
Washington DC 20036-1206
(202) 667-9700
(202) 667-8629 (fax)
http://www.nafcm.org

The National Clearinghouse on Child Abuse and Neglect Information

The National Clearinghouse on Child Abuse and Neglect Information and the National Adoption Information Clearinghouse are services of the Children's Bureau, Administration for Children and Families, U.S. Department of Health and Human Services. The mission of the Clearinghouses is to connect professionals and concerned citizens to practical, timely, and essential information on programs, research, legislation, and statistics to promote the safety, permanency, and well-being of children and families.

National Clearinghouse on Child Abuse and Neglect Information
330 C Street SW
Washington, DC 20447
(800) 394-3366 or (703)385-7565
(703) 385-3206 (fax)
http://nccanch.acf.hhs.gov

National Data Archive on Child Abuse and Neglect (NDACAN)

A resource since 1988, NDACAN promotes scholarly exchange among researchers in the child maltreatment field. NDACAN acquires microdata from leading researchers and national data collection efforts and makes these datasets available to the research community for secondary analysis. NDACAN supports information sharing through its electronic mailing list and Updata newsletter and provides training opportunities to researchers through conference workshops and its annual Summer Research Institute.

National Data Archive on Child Abuse and Neglect
Beebe Hall—FLDC
Cornell University
Ithaca NY 14853
(607) 255-7799
(607) 255-8562 (fax)
http://www.ndacan.cornell.edu

National Directory of Children, Youth, and Family Services

"The National Directory of Children, Youth, and Family Services is the *#1 resource* used by professionals assisting at-risk children, youth and their families." The Directory networks professionals with your colleagues, more than 50,000 key contacts in the areas of social services, health and mental services, juvenile justice agencies, education departments, treatment centers and hospitals, adoption and foster care agencies, referral networks, and more.

National Directory of CYF Services
14 Inverness Drive East, Suite D144
Englewood, CO 80112
(800) 343-6681
(800) 845-6452 (fax)
http:/www.childrenyouthfamilydir.com

Child Trends

Child Trends is a 25-year-old nonprofit, nonpartisan research organization dedicated to improving the lives of children by conducting research and providing science-based information to improve the decisions, programs, and policies that affect children and their families.

Child Trends
4301 Connecticut Avenue NW, Suite 100
Washington, DC 20008
(202) 572-6000
(202) 362-8420 (fax)
http://www.childtrends.org

Family and Youth Services Bureau (FYSB)

FYSB supports local communities in providing services and opportunities to young people, particularly runaway and homeless youth. FYSB does so by awarding funding that enables communities to offer services to young people and their families and to test new approaches to helping youth. In addition, the bureau has created a network of support that includes a national hotline and referral system for runaway and homeless youth; offers conferences, trainings, and onsite consultations; documents effective practices; and distributes information.

Administration for Children and Families
370 L'Enfant Promenade SW
Washington, DC 20447
http://www.acf.hhs.gov/programs/fysb

The National Clearinghouse on Families and Youth (NCFY)

NCFY has links to information that will help you support young people and families.

National Clearinghouse on Families and Youth
P.O. Box 13505
Silver Spring, MD 20911-3505
(301) 608-8098
(301) 608-8721 (fax)
info@ncfy.com
http://www.ncfy.com

Children's Defense Fund

"The Mission of Children's Defense Fund is to Leave No Child Behind and to ensure every child a healthy start, a head start, a fair start, a safe start, and a moral start in life as successful passage to adulthood with the help of caring families and communities."

Children's Defense Fund
25 E Street NW
Washington, DC 20001
(202) 628-8787
cdfinfo@childrensdefense.org
http://www.childrensdefense.org

National Institute on Drug Abuse (NIDA)

NIDA's mission is to lead the nation in bringing the power of science to bear on drug abuse and addiction. Recent scientific advances have revolutionized our understanding of drug abuse and addiction. The majority of these advances, which have dramatic implications for how to best prevent and treat addiction, have been supported by NIDA. NIDA supports over 85 percent of the world's research on the health aspects of drug abuse and addiction. NIDA-supported science addresses the most fundamental and essential questions about drug abuse, ranging from the molecule to managed care and from DNA to community outreach research.

National Institute on Drug Abuse
National Institutes of Health
6001 Executive Boulevard, Room 5213
Bethesda, MD 20892-9561
http://www.nida.nih.gov

American Professional Society on the Abuse of Children (APSAC)

APSAC is a nonprofit national organization focused on meeting the needs of professionals engaged in all aspects of services for maltreated children and their families. Especially important to APSAC is the dissemination of state-of-the-art practice in all professional disciplines related to child abuse and neglect.

APSAC
P.O. Box 30669
Charleston, SC 29417
(877) 40A-PSAC
(803) 753-9823 (fax)
http://apsac.fmhi.usf.edu

KidsPeace

KidsPeace is a private, not-for-profit charity dedicated to serving the critical behavioral and mental health needs of children, preadolescents, and teens. Since 1882, KidsPeace has been helping kids develop the confidence and skills they need to overcome crisis. KidsPeace provides specialized residential treatment services and a comprehensive range of treatment programs and educational services to help families help kids anticipate and avoid crisis whenever possible.

KidsPeace National Centers of New England
P.O. Box 787
Route 180
Ellsworth, ME 04605
(800) 992-9KID
http://www.kidspeace.org

National Center for Children Exposed to Violence (NCCEV)

It is the mission of NCCEV to increase the capacity of individuals and communities to reduce the incidence and impact of violence on children and families; to train and support the professionals who provide intervention and treatment to children and families affected by violence; and to increase professional and public awareness of the effects of violence on children, families, communities and society.

National Center for Children Exposed to Violence
Yale University Child Study Center
230 South Frontage Road
New Haven, CT 06520-7900
(877) 49NCCEV
http://www.nccev.org

National Youth Development Information Center (NYDIC)

NYDIC is a website for youth workers with interest in any of the following areas: funding, programming, research, policy, job and training opportunities. NYDIC also provides current news to the youth development field.

National Collaboration for Youth
1319 F Street NW, Suite 601
Washington, DC 20004
(877) NYDIC-4-U
(202) 393-4517 (fax)
http://www.nydic.org

Bibliography and Readings

1992 Child Abuse and Neglect Report. (1992). Madison, WI: Bureau for Children, Youth and Families, Division of Community Services, Wisconsin Department of Health and Social Services.

2002–2003 Pride Surveys National Summary (2003). Bowling Green, KY: Pride Questionnaire Report for Grades 6 thru 12.

Banks, J. A. (1997). *Educating Citizens in a Multicultural Society.* Williston, VT: Teachers College Press.

Barnett, W. S. (1993). Economic evaluation of home visiting programs. *The Future of Children,* 3 (3): 93–112.

Barr, R. and Parrett, W. (2003). *Saving Our Students—Saving Our Schools: 50 Proven Strategies.* Glenview, IL: Skylight Professional Development Publishing.

Beck, E. L. (1999). Prevention and intervention programming: Lessons from an after-school program. *The Urban Review,* 31(1): 107–124.

Benard, B. (1997). *Turning It Around for All Youth: From Risk to Resilience.* New York: ERIC Clearinghouse on Urban Education, ERIC/CUE Digest No. 126.

Benson, P. L., Galbraith, J., and Espeland, P. (1998). *What Kids Need to Succeed.* Minneapolis, MN: Free Spirit. ED423 076.

Bermudez, A. B. (1994). Doing our homework: How schools can engage Hispanic communities. Charleston, WV: The ERIC Clearinghouse on Rural Education and Small Schools.

Berube, M. R. (1983). Educating the urban poor. *The Urban Review,* 15(3): 151–163.

Bettis, P. (1996). Urban abstraction in a central city high school. *The Urban Review,* 28(4): 309–335.

Bickart, T. S. and Wolin, S. (1997). Practicing resilience in the elementary classroom. *Principal,* 77(2): 21–25.

Bishop, J. Eric and Fransen, Sharon. (1998). Building community: An alternative assessment. *Phi Delta Kappan,* 80(1), September: 39–40.

Blakemore, C. (1998). *A Public School of Your Own.* Golden, CO: Adams-Pomeroy Press.

Boers, D. (2002). *Lost and Found: CARTIE Classrooms for Reclaiming Students.* Lanham, MD: University Press of America, Inc.

Bradshaw, J. (1988). *Bradshaw On: The Family.* Deerfield Beach, FL: Health Communications, Inc.

Bradshaw, J. (1988). *Healing the Shame That Binds You.* Deerfield Beach, FL: Health Communications, Inc.

Brewer, D. J., and Gray, M. J. (1999). Do faculty connect school to work? Evidence from community colleges. *Educational Evaluation and Policy Analysis,* 21(4): 405–416.

Bruner, C. (1993). *Toward Outcome-Based Accountability: Readings on Constructing Cost-of-Failure/Return on Investment Analysis of Prevention Initiatives.* Des Moines, IA: Child and Family Policy Center.

Bruner, C. (1996). *Potential Returns on Investment from a Comprehensive Family Center Approach in High-Risk Neighborhoods: Background Paper, Allegheny County Study.* Des Moines, IA: Child and Family Policy Center.

Bruner, C. and Scott, S. (1994). *Investment-Based Budgeting—The Principles in Converting from a Remediation Response to a Prevention/Investment Budget. Occasional Paper #11.* Des Moines, IA: Child and Family Policy Center.

Caldwell, R. A. (1992). *The Cost of Child Abuse vs. Child Abuse Prevention: Michigan's Experience.* East Lansing, MI: Michigan Children's Trust Fund.

Cantelon, S. and LeBoeuf, D. (1997). Keeping young people in school: Community programs that work. OJJDP: *Juvenile Justice Bulletin.* June: 1–11.

Carpenter-Aeby, T., Salloum, M., and Aeby, V. G. (2001). A process evaluation of school social work services in a disciplinary alternative education program. *Children & Schools,* 23 (3): 171–181.

Catalano, R. F, Berglund, M. L., Ryan, J. A., Lonczak, H., and Hawkins, J. (2002). Defining and evaluating positive youth development. *Prevention & Treatment,* Volume 5, Article 15, Washington, DC: American Psychologial Association.

Child Welfare of America (CWA) (1997). State agency survey. Washington, D.C.: CWA.

Christman, J., et al. (1997). Growing smaller: Three tasks in restructuring urban high schools. *Urban Education,* 32(1): 146–165.

Conrath, J. (1994). *You, Youth, Responsibility, and Self Control.* Lopez Island, WA: Our Other Youth.

A Coordinated Response to Child Abuse and Neglect: A Basic Manual. (1992). U.S. Department of Health and Human Services, Administration for Children and Families. DHHS Publication No. (ACF) 92-30362. McLean, VA: The Circle, Inc.

Corbett, H. D. and Wilson, B. L. (1998). Scaling within rather than scaling up: Implications from students' experiences in reforming urban middle schools. *The Urban Review,* 30(4): 261–293.

Courtney, M. E. (1998). The costs of child protection in the context of welfare reform. *Future of Children,* 8(1): 88–103.

Cox, S. M. (1999). An assessment of an alternative education program for at-risk delinquent youth. *Journal of Research in Crime & Delinquency,* 36 (3): 323–336.

Dallas Commission on Children and Youth. (1988). *A Step Towards a Business Plan for Children in Dallas County: Technical Report Child Abuse and Neglect.* Dallas: Community Council of Greater Dallas, TX.

Dallmann-Jones, A. (2006). *Handbook of Effective Teaching and Assessment Strategies, 2nd ed.* Lancaster, PA: RLD Publications.

Dallmann-Jones, A. (1996). Resolving Unfinished Business: *Assessing the Effects of Being Raised in a Dysfunctional Environment.* Fond du Lac, WI: Three Blue Herons Publishing.

Daro, D. (1988). *Confronting Child Abuse*: Research for Effective Program Design. New York: The Free Press, Macmillian, Inc.

Dembo, M. H. and Eaton, M. J. (2000). Self-regulation of academic learning in middle-level schools. *The Elementary School Journal*, 100(5): 473–490.

Dicintio, M. J. and Gee, S. (1999). Control is the key: unlocking the motivation of at-risk students. *Psychology in the Schools*, 36(3) 231–237.

Doll, B. and Hess, R. S. (2001). Through a new lens: contemporary psychological perspectives on school completion and dropping out of high school. *School Psychology Quarterly*, 16 (4): 351–356.

Dryfoos, J. G. (1997) The prevalence of problem behaviors: Implications for programs. In: *Healthy Children 2010: Enhancing Children's Wellness* (pp. 17–46). Thousand Oaks, CA: Sage.

Dubowitz, H. (1990). Costs and effectiveness of interventions in child maltreatment. *Child Abuse and Neglect*, 14(2): 177–186.

Dugger, C. W. and Desmoulin-Kherat, S. (1996). Helping younger dropouts get back into school. *Middle School Journal*, 28 (November): 29–33.

Duke, D. J. and Griesdorn, J. (1999). Considerations in the design of alternative schools. *Clearing House*, 73 (2): 89–92.

Dyson, B., and O'Sullivan, M. (1998). Innovation in two alternative elementary school programs: why it works. *Research Quarterly for Exercise & Sport*, 69(3): 242–253.

Editor. (2001). *Population Estimates and Projections: Understanding Census 2000. Race Category Changes and Comparisons*. Olympia, WA: Washington State Office of Financial Management.

Esters, I. (2003). Salient worries of at-risk youth: Needs assessment using the things I worry about scale. *Adolescence*. June 22: 45–47.

Every Child Matters Education Fund Annual Report, (2003). *How Federal Budget Priorities and Tax Cuts Are Harming America's Children*. Washington, DC: Every Child Matters.

Farber, P. (1998). *Small Schools Work Best for Disadvantaged Students*. The Harvard Education Letter.

Farmer S. (2002). *Sacred Ceremonies*. Carlsbad, CA: Hay House, Inc.

Farmer, S. (1992). *Healing Words*. New York: Ballantine.

Farmer, S. (1991). The Wounded Male. New York: Bantam Books.

Farmer, S. (1989). *Adult Children of Abusive Parents*. Los Angeles, CA: Lowell House Legacy.

Fashola, O. S., Slavin, R, and Colderon, M. (1997). *Effective Programs for Latino Students in Elementary and Middle Schools*. Baltimore, MD: Johns Hopkins University.

Fashola, O. S. and Slavin, R. E. (1997). Effective dropout prevention and college attendance programs for Latino students. Hispanic dropout project. *Educational Leadership*, 44(6): 19–21.

Finn, C. (2000). *Charter Schools in Action: Renewing Public Education*. Princeton, NJ: Princeton University Press.

Finn, J. D. (1998). *Class Size and Students at Risk: What Is Known? What Is Next?* National Institute on the Education of At-Risk Students, Office of Educational Research and Improvement. Washington, DC: US Department of Education.

Forward, S. (1989). *Toxic Parents—Overcoming Their Hurtful Legacy and Reclaiming Your Life*. New York: Bantam.

Fossum, M. and Mason M. (1986). *Facing Shame: Families in Recovery*. New York: W.W. Norton and Company.

Franey, K., Geffner, R., and Falconer, R., (eds.). (2001). *The Cost of Child Maltreatment: Who Pays? We All Do*. San Diego, CA: Family Violence & Sexual Assault Institute.

Friel, J. C. & Friel, L. (1988). *Adult Children: The Secrets of Dysfunctional Families*. Health Communications, Inc.

Gandara, P. and Chavez, L. (2000). *Putting the Cart before the Horse: Latinos and Higher Education.* Davis and Berkeley, CA: University of California.

Gannon, J. (1989). *Soul Survivors.* New York: Prentice Hall Press.

Garbarino, J. (1980). Some thoughts on school size and its effects on adolescent development. *Journal of Youth and Adolescence*, 9(1): 19–31.

Garry, E. (1996). *Truancy: First Step to a Lifetime of Problems.* Washington, DC: Office of Juvenile Justice and Delinquency Prevention.

Geen, R., Waters, S., Tumlin, K. C., and Boots, S. W. (1999). *The Cost of Protecting Vulnerable Children: Understanding Federal, State, and Local Child Welfare Spending.* New York: The Urban Institute.

Gil, E. (1988). *Treatment of Adult Survivors of Childhood Abuse.* Fairfax, VA: Launch Press.

Giovannoni, J. and Becerra, R. (1979). *Defining Child Abuse.* NewYork: The Free Press, Macmillan Publishing Co., Inc.

Gomez, B. (1996). Service-learning and school-to-work strategies for revitalizing urban education and communities. *Education and Urban Society*, 28(2): 160–166.

Gottfredson, D. C. (1990). Changing school structures to benefit high-risk youths. In: P. E. Leone (ed.), *Understanding Troubled and Troubling Youth*, (pp. 246–271). Newbury Park, CA: Sage.

Gould, M. S. and O'Brien, T. (1995). *Child Maltreatment in Colorado: The Value of Prevention and the Cost of Failure to Prevent.* Denver, CO: Center for Human Investment Policy, University of Colorado at Denver.

Green, J. (2002). *The GED Myth.* NewYork: Manhattan Institute for Public Policy Research.

Gregg, S. (1999). Creating effective alternatives for disruptive students. *The Clearing House*, 73(2): 107–113.

Gregory, T. (2001). Fear of success? Ten ways alternative schools pull their punches. *Phi Delta Kappan*, 82 (8): 577–582.

Gross, B. (1990). Here dropouts drop in—and stay! *Phi Delta Kappan*, 71(April): 625–627.

Groth, C. (1998). Dumping ground or effective alternative: dropout-prevention programs in urban schools. *Urban Education*, 33(2): 218–242.

Grunbaum, J. A., Kann, L., Kinchen, S. A., Ross, J. G., Gowda, V. R., Collins, J. L., and Kolbe, L. J. (2000). Youth risk behavior surveillance national alternative high school youth risk behavior survey, United States, 1998. *Journal of School Health*, 70(1): 5–17.

Grunbaum, J. A., Lowry, R., and Kann, L. (2001). Prevalence of health-related behaviors among alternative high school students as compared with students attending regular high schools. *Journal of Adolescent Health*, 29 (5): 337–343.

Guerin, G. and Denti, L. G. (1999). Alternative education support for youth at-risk. *The Clearing House*, 73(2): 76–78.

Spring, J. (2001). *Deculturalization and the struggle for equality: A Brief History of the Education of Dominated Cultures in the United States.* Boston: McGraw-Hill.

Guindon, J. (1992). *Developing an In-School Suspension Program in an Elementary School as an Alternative to Home-Bound Suspension.* ERIC Accession Number ED349679.

Haertel, G. D. and Wang, M. C. (Eds.). (1997). *Coordination, Cooperation, Collaboration: What We Know about School-Linked Services.* Laboratory for Student Success: The Mid-Atlantic Regional Educational Laboratory. Philadelphia, PA: Temple University Center for Research in Human Development and Education.

Hammer, B. (2003). Charter schools produce higher test scores, but segregated environment: recent studies assess race, academic achievement in the nation's charter schools (study by Manhattan Institute). *Black Issues in Higher Education,* August 28: 4–6.

Hammerle (1992), as cited in Myles, K. T. (2001). Disabilities Caused by Child Maltreatment: *Incidence, Prevalence and Financial Data.* "Briefing Report for the New Mexico Family Impact Seminar" (p. 28). Las Cruces, NM: New Mexico State University.

Hammerle (1992). as cited in Daro, D. (1988). *Confronting Child Abuse.* New York: The Free Press.

Hamovitch, B. (1999). More failure for the disadvantaged: Contradictory African-American student reactions to compensatory education and urban schooling. *The Urban Review,* 31(1): 55–77.

HCUPnet (2000). Available on-line at http://www.ahrq.gov/data/hcup/hcupnet.htm.

Hellriegel, K. L. and Yates, J. R. (1999). Collaboration between correctional and public school systems serving juvenile offenders: a case study. *Education & Treatment of Children,* 22 (1): 55–83.

Henderson, N. (1997). Resiliency in schools: Making it happen. *Principal,* 77(2): 10–17.

Henley, P., Fuston, J. and Peters, T. (2000). Rescuing elementary school troublemakers. *The Education Digest,* 65(8): 48–52.

Heubert, J. (ed.). (1999). *Law and School Reform: Six Strategies for Promoting Educational Equity.* New Haven, CT: Yale University Press.

Hill, H. M. and Jones, L. P. (1997). Children's and parents' perceptions of children's exposure to violence in urban neighborhoods." *Journal of the National Medical Association,* 89(4): 270–276.

Holloway, J. H. (2000) Extracurricular activities: The path to academic success? *Educational Leadership,* 57(4): 87–88.

Horn, L. J., and Chen, X. (1998). *Toward Resiliency: At Risk Students Who Make It to College.* Washington, DC: U.S. Department of Education, Office of Educational Research and Improvement.

Huxley, A. (1962). *Island.* New York: Bantam Books.

Ingersoll, S. & LeBoeuf, D. (1997). Reaching out to youth out of the education (traditional) mainstream and current (alternative) school environments. *High School Journal,* 85 (2), 12–23.

Johnson, S. T., Thompson, S. D., Wallace, M. B., Hughes, G. B. and Manswell-Butly, J. L. (1998). How teachers and university faculty perceive the need for and importance of professional development in performance-based assessment. *Journal of Negro Education,* 67(3): 197–210.

Jones, D. L. and Sandidge, R. F. (1997). Recruiting and retaining teachers in urban schools. *Education and Urban Society,* 29(2): 192–203.

Jones, P. A. (1991). Educating black males: Several solutions. *Crisis,* 98(8): 12–18.

Justice Research & Statistics Association. (1995). *Youth, Drugs and Violence: Results from State and Local Program Workshops.* Office of Justice Programs, U.S. Department of Justice.

Kallio, B. R. and Sanders, E. T. W. (1999). An alternative school collaboration model. *American Secondary Education,* 28(2): 27–36.

Kaplan, E. B. (1999). "It's going good": Inner-city Black and Latino adolescents' perceptions about achieving an education. *Urban Education,* 34(2): 181–213.

Kapp, D. R. and Breslin, B. (2001). Restorative justice in school communities. *Youth & Society,* 33 (2): 249–272.

Katsiyannis, A., Kearney, N. E. and Williams, B. (1998). A national survey of state initiatives on alternative education. *Remedial & Special Education,* 19 (5): 276–284.

Keith, N. Z. (1996). Can urban school reform and community development be joined? *Education and Urban Society*, 28(2): 237–268.

Kelley, B. T., Thornberry, T. P. and Smith, C. A. (1997). *In the Wake of Childhood Violence.* Washington, DC: National Institute of Justice.

Kellmayer, J. (1995). Educating chronically disruptive and disaffected high school students. *NASSP Bulletin*, 79(Jan.): 82–87.

Kellmayer, J. (1998). Building educational alternatives for at-risk youth: a primer. *High School Magazine*, 6(2): 26–31.

Kellogg, T. (1990). *Broken Toys, Broken Dreams.* Amherst, MA: Brat Publishing.

Kelly, J. P. (1997). Experiences in a juvenile justice system. *Social Education*, 61(Sept.): 268–269.

Kelley, B. T., Thornberry, T. P., and Smith, C. A. (1997). In the Wake of Childhood Maltreatment. Juvenile Justice Bulletin. Office of Juvenile Justice and Delinquency Prevention. U.S. Dept. of Justice. Washington, D.C. (August): 23–29.

Knutson, J. (1998). A second chance: alternative high schools take different approaches. *Educational Horizons*, 76 (4): 199–202.

Kozol, J. (1992). *Savage inequalities: Children in America's Schools.* New York: Harper Perennial.

Lamperes, B (1994). Empowering at-risk students to succeed. *Educational Leadership*, 52(Nov.): 67–70.

Lange, C. M. (1998). Characteristics of alternative schools and programs serving at-risk students. *The High School Journal*, 81(4):183–198.

LaPoint, V., Jordan, W., McPartland, J. M., and Towns, D. P. (1996). *The Talent Development High School: Essential Components.* Report No. 1. Washington, DC: Center for Research on the Education of Students Placed at Risk.

LeBoeuf, D. (1997). *Reaching Out to Youth Out of the Mainstream.* Office of Juvenile Justice and Delinquency Prevention.

Lee, P. W. (1999). In their own voices: An ethnographic study of low-achieving students within the context of school reform. *Urban Education*, 34(2): 214–244.

Legters, N. E. (1999). *Teacher Collaboration in a Restructuring Urban High School.* Baltimore, MD: Johns Hopkins University.

Leone, P. E. and Drakeford, W. (1999). Alternative education: from a "last chance" to a proactive model. *Clearing House*, 3(2): 86–88.

Leventhal, T. and Brooks-Gunn, J. (2000). The neighborhoods they live in: The effects of neighborhood residence on child and adolescent outcomes. *Psychological Bulletin*, 126(2): 309–337.

Levin, H. M. (1988). *Accelerated Schools for Children at Risk.* Research Report Series RR-0010. New Brunswick, NJ: Rutgers University Center for Policy Research in Education.

Levine, E. (2002). One kid at a time: Big lessons from a small school. *Series on School Reform.* Phi Delta Kappan, 72(7): 550–554.

Lew, M. (1990). *Victims No Longer.* St. Helens, OR: Perennial Press.

Linker, J. and Marion, B. (1995). *A Study of the Effects of Options, an Alternative Educational Program, on the Personal Success of At-Risk Students: A Five Year Study.* ERIC Accession Number ED398338.

Linton, E. P (2000). Alternative schooling for troubled youth in rural communities. *School Administrator*, v. 57(2): 46.

Liontos, L. B. (1991). *Social Services and Schools: Building Collaboration That Works.* Eugene, OR: Oregon School Study Council. OSSC Bulletin Series.

Lloyd, D. L. (1997). From high school to middle school: an alternative school program for both. *The Education Digest*, 62 (Mar.): 32–35.

Lockwood, A. T. and Secada, W.G. (1999). *Transforming Education for Hispanic Youth: Exemplary Practices, Programs, and Schools*. Washington, D.C., Center for the Study of Language and Education, The George Washington University.

Loeber, R. and Stouthamer-Loeber, M. (1987). Predcition. In *Handbook of Juvenile Delinquency*, edited by H. C. Quay. New York: Wiley, pp. 325–382.

MacIver, D. J., Balfanz, R., and Plank, S. (1998). *An Elective Replacement Approach to Providing Extra Help in Math—The CATAMA Program* (Computer- and Team-Assisted Mathematics Program). Report No. 21. Baltimore, MD: Center for Research on Education of Students Placed at Risk.

Martínez, Y. G., and Velázquez, J. A. (2000). *Involving Migrant Families in Education*. ERIC Clearinghouse on Rural Education and Small Schools, ERIC Digest EDORC-00-4.

Mascow, A. (1971). *The Farther Reaches of Human Nature*. New York; Viking Press.

McCarthey, S. (1999). Identifying teacher practices that connect home and school. *Education and Urban Society*, 32(1): 83–107.

McDonald, L. and Sayger, T. (1998). Impact of a family and school-based program on protective factors for high risk youth. *Drugs and Society*, 12(1–2).

McGee, J. (2001). Reflections of an alternative school administrator. *Phi Delta Kappan*, 82 (8): 588–592.

Melaville, A. (1998). *Learning together: The Developing Field of School–Community Initiatives*. Institute for Educational Leadership and National Center for Community Education. Flint, MI: Mott Foundation.

Melbourne, F. H., Blumberg, E. J., Liles, S., Powell, L., Morrison, T. C., Duran, G., Sipan, C.L., Burkhamd, S., and Kelley, N. (2001). Training AIDS and anger prevention social skills in at-risk adolescents. *Journal of Counseling & Development*, 79: 347–355.

Merrill, S. A. (1999). Roselawn: A community regaining its youth. *The Clearing House*, 73(2): 101–103.

Middleton-Moz, J. (1989). *Children of Trauma*. Deerfield Beach, FL: Health Communications, Inc.

Miller, A. (1981). *The Drama of the Gifted Child*. New York: Basic Books, Inc.

Miller, A. (1988). *For Your Own Good*. New York: Farrar Straus Giroux.

Miller, A. (1998). "The childhood trauma." Lecture at the Lexington 92nd Street YWCA, New York City.

Miller, T., Cohen, M. and Wiersema, B. (1996). *Victims Cost and Consequences: A New Look*. Washington, D.C.: The National Institute of Justice.

Mirel, J. and Angus, D. (1999). *The Failed Promise of the American High School*. New York: Teachers College Press.

Missouri Children's Trust Fund (1997). *The Economic Costs of Shaken Baby Syndrome Survivors in Missouri*. Jefferson City, MO: Missouri Children's Trust Fund.

Moats, L. C. (1998). Teaching decoding. *American Educator*, 22(1): 42–49, 95–96. Spring-Summer.

Myers, J. E. B., Berliner, L., Briere, J., and Hendrix, C. T., Myers, E. B., Finklethor, D., and Berliner, L. (2001). *The APSAC Handbook on Child Maltreatment, Second Edition*. Thousand Oaks, CA: Sage Publications, Inc.

National At-Risk Education Network (NAREN) (2004). *Nine Facets of Quality At-Risk Education*. Fond du Lac, WI: National At-Risk Education Network.

National Commission on Teaching and America's Future. (1996). *What Matters Most: Teaching for America's Future.* Woodbridge, VA: The National Commission on Teaching and America's Future.

National Research Council. (1993). *Understanding Child Abuse and Neglect.* Washington, DC: National Academy Press.

Thakur, M. (ed.). (2002). *NYEC EDNet Tools for Transformational Education.* Washington DC: National Youth Employment Coalition.

Olds, D. and Kitzman, H. (1993). *Review of research on home visiting for pregnant women and parents of young children. The Future of Children,* 3(3): 53–92.

Olds, D. L., Henderson, C. R., Phelps, C., Kitzman, H., and Hanks, C. (1993). Effect of prenatal and infancy nurse home visitation on government spending. *Medical Care,* 31(2): 155–174.

Oxley, D. (1993). *Organizing schools into Smaller Units:* A Planning Guide. Publication 931. Philadelphia, PA: National Center on Education in the Inner Cities at the Temple University Center for Research in Human Development and Education.

Oxley, D. and McCabe, J. G. (1989). *Making Big High Schools Smaller.* New York: Public Education Association.

Paglin, C. and Fager, J. (1997). *Alternative Schools: Approaches for Students at Risk.* Portland, OR: Northwest Regional Educational Laboratory.

Peck, S. (1983). *People of the Lie.* New York; Touchstone.

Peterson, R. L. & Smith, C. R. (2002). Dealing with behaviors perceived as unacceptable in schools: The interim alternative education program. *Addressing the Diverse Needs of Children and Youth with Emotional-Behavioral Disorders—Programs That Work.* Alexandria, VA: The Council for Children with Behavioral Disorders.

Petit, M. R. and Curtis, P. (1997). *Child Abuse and Neglect: A Look at the States.* 1997 CWLA Stat Book. Washington, DC: CWLA Press.

Pisano, L. E. (1994). A charter school for at-risk kids. *The Education Digest,* 59 (Jan.): 64–66.

Plotnick, R. D. and Deppman, L. (1999). Using benefit-cost analysis to assess child abuse prevention and intervention programs. *Child Welfare* 78(3): 381–407.

Pulido, J. A. (1995). A high school program for "at risk" Latino youth: Mujeres y Hombres Nobles (Honorable Men and Women). *American Secondary Education,* 23(2): 10–12.

Purcell-Gates, V. (1995). *Other People's Words: The Cycle of Low Literacy.* Cambridge, MA: Harvard University Press.

Ravitch, D. (2000). *Left Back: A Century of Failed School Reforms.* New York: Simon & Schuster.

Renzulli, J. S. (1998). A rising tide lifts all ships: Developing the gifts and talents of all students. *Phi Delta Kappan,* 80(2): 104–111.

Reyes, O., Kobus, K., and Gillock, K. (1999). Career aspirations of urban, Mexican American adolescent females. *Hispanic Journal of Behavioral Sciences,* 21(3): 366–382.

Reyes, P. and Capper, C. A. (1991). Urban principals: A critical perspective on the context of minority student dropout. *Educational Administration Quarterly,* 27(4): 530–557.

Rivera, L. (2003). Changing women: An ethnographic study of homeless mothers and popular education. *Journal of Sociology and Social Welfare,* June: 45–60.

Rodenstein, J. M. (1990). *Children at Risk: A Resource and Planning Guide.* Madison, WI: Wisconsin Department of Public Instruction.

Rodriguez-Brown, F. V., Li, Ran-Fery, Albom, J. B. (1999). Hispanic parents' awareness and use of literacy-rich environments at home and in the community. *Education and Urban Society,* 32(1): 41–58.

Rogers, C. R. and Freiberg, H. J. (1994). *Freedom to Learn.* 3rd ed. Columbus: Prentice Hall.

Romo, H. D. (1999). *Reaching Out: Best Practices for Educating Mexican-Origin Children and Youth*. Charleston, WV: The ERIC Clearinghouse on Rural Education and Small Schools.

Sagor, R. (1999). Equity and excellence in public schools: The role of the alternative school. *Clearing House*, 73(2): 72–76.

Sakayi, D. N. R. (2001). Intellectual indignation: getting at the roots of student resistance in an alternative high school program. *Education*, 122 (2): 414–423.

Samenow, S. (1989). *Before It's Too Late*. New York: Random House—Times Books.

Sanders, M. G. and Epstein, J. L. (1998). *School–Family–Community Partnerships in Middle and High Schools: From Theory to Practice*. Report No. 22. Baltimore, MD: Center for Research on the Education of Students Placed at Risk.

Sanders, M. G. (1997). *Building Effective School–Family–Community Partnerships in a Large Urban School District*. Baltimore, MD: Johns Hopkins University.

Schargel, F. (2003). *Dropout Prevention Tools*. Larchmont, NY: Eye on Education.

Schargel, F. (2004). *Helping Students Graduate: A Strategic Approach to Dropout Prevention*. Larchmont, NY: Eye on Education.

Schargel, F. and Smink, J. (2001). *Strategies to Help Solve Our School Dropout Problem*. Larchmont, NY: Eye on Education.

Scheurich, J. J. (1998). Highly successful and loving, public elementary schools populated mainly by low-SES children of color. *Urban Education*, 33(4): 151–491.

Schwartz, W. (1997). School dropouts: new information about an old problem. *ERIC Digest 109*. ERIC Clearinghouse on Urban Education.

Schwartz, W. (2001). *Strategies for Improving the Educational Outcomes of Latinas*. ERIC Clearinghouse on Urban Education, ERIC Digest EDO-UD-01-6.

Sedlak, A. and Broadhurst, D. (1996). *The Third National Incidence Study of Child Abuse and Neglect: NIS 3*. U.S. Department of Health and Human Services.

Slavin, R. E. and Fashola, O. S. (1998). *Show Me the Evidence! Proven and Promising Programs for America's Schools*. Center for Research on the Education of Students Placed at Risk. Thousand Oaks, CA: Corwin Press.

Smith, A. (1988.) *Grandchildren of Alcoholics*. Deerfield Beach, FL: Health Communications, Inc.

Smith, S. and Thomases, J. (2001). *CBO Schools: Profiles in Transformational Education*. Washington, DC: AED Center for Youth Development and Policy Research.

Snow, C. E., Burns, M. S., and Griffin, P. (eds.) (1998). *Preventing Reading Difficulties in Young Children*. Committee on the Prevention of Reading Difficulties, National Research Council. Washington, DC: National Academy Press.

Solo, L., Sr. (1992). Getting support from the community. *Principal*, 71 (Jan.): 26–27.

Special Edition. (1995). Second-chance schools. *Executive Educator*, 17 (Mar.): 27–29.

Spring, J. (1996). *The Cultural Transformation of a Native American Family and Its Tribe, 1763–1995: A Basket of Apples*. Mahwah, NJ: Lawrence Erlbaum Associates.

Spring, J. (1998). *Conflict of Interests: The Politics of American Education*. Boston, MA: McGraw-Hill.

Spring, J. (2000). *The Universal Right to Education: Justification, Definition, and Guidelines*. Mahwah, NJ: Lawrence Erlbaum Associates.

Stern, D., Raby, M., and Dayton, C. (1992). *Career Academies: Partnerships for Reconstructing American High Schools*. San Francisco, CA: Jossey-Bass.

Sutton, J., Smith, P. K., and Swettenham, J. (1999). Bullying and 'theory of mind': a critique of the 'social skills deficit' view of anti-social behavior. *Social Development*, 8(1): 117–127.

Sylvester, P. S. (1994). Elementary school curricula and urban transformation. *Harvard Educational Review*, 64(3): 309–331.

Taylor-Dunlop, K. and Norton, M. M. (1997). Out of the mouths of babes: Voices of at-risk adolescents. *The Clearing House*, 70 (May/June): 274–278.

Tharp, R. and Gallimore, R. (1988). *Rousing Minds to Life: Teaching, Learning and Schooling in Social Context*. New York: Cambridge University Press.

Tobin, T. and Sprague, J. (2000). Alternative education strategies: reducing violence in school and the community. *Journal of Emotional & Behavioral Disorders*, 8(3): 177–187.

Tolan, P. and Guerra, N. (1994). *What Works in Reducing Adolescent Violence: An Empirical Review of the Field*. Boulder, CO: Center for the Study and Prevention of Violence.

Trends to watch: 1998 and beyond. Washington DC: *Readers Digest*. Ministry Development Division.

U.S. Census 2000. Available online at www.census.gov.

U.S. Census 2004. Available online at www.census.gov.

U.S. General Accounting Office (1992). *Child Abuse: Prevention Programs Need Greater Emphasis*. Washington, DC: GAO .

U.S. General Accounting Office Publication. (2002). *School Dropouts. Education Could Play a Stronger Role in Identifying and Disseminating Promising Prevention Strategies*. Publication GAO-02-240, p. 16.

U.S. Surgeon General Office (1999). *Mental Illness in Children of United States*.

Vanderslice, R. (1999). Developing effective in-school suspension programs. *The Delta Kappa Gamma Bulletin*, 65(4): Summer: 33–38.

Vann, M., Schubert, S. R., and Rogers, D. (2000). The Big Bayou Association: An alternative education program for middle school at-risk juveniles. *Preventing School Failure*, 45(1): 31–37.

Vernez, G., Krop, R. A., and Rydell, C. P. (1999). *Closing the Education Gap: Benefits and Costs*. Los Angeles, CA: RAND Institute.

Walker, F, Unutzer, J., Rutter, C., Gelfand, A. Saunders, K., VonKorff, M. Koss, M. and Katon, W. (1997). *Cost of health care use by women HMO members with a history of childhood abuse and neglect*. Arc General Psychiatry, 56: 609–613.

Walker, H. M. and Golly, A. (1999). Developing behavioral alternatives for antisocial children at the point of school entry. *The Clearing House*, 73(2): 104–106.

Walters, D. (1975). *Physical and Sexual Abuse of Children: Causes and Treatment*. Bloomington, IN: Indiana University Press.

Wasik, B. A. and Slavin, R. E. (1990). *Preventing Early Reading Failure with One-to-One Tutoring: A Best-Evidence Synthesis*. Report No. 6. Baltimore: Center for Research on Effective Schooling for Disadvantaged Students.

Watt, D. L. Roessingh, H., and Bosetti, L. (1996). Success and failure: Stories of ESL students' educational and cultural adjustment to high school. *Urban Education*, 31(2): 199–221.

Wehlage, G. G., Rutter, R. A., Smith, G. A., Lesko, N., and Fernandez, R. R. (1989). *Reducing the Risk: Schools as Communities of Support*. Philadelphia, PA: Falmer.

Weiner, L., Leighton, M. & Funkhouser, J. (2000). *Helping Hispanic Students Reach High Academic Standards: An Idea Book*. U.S. Dept. of Education.

Weir, R. M. (1996). Lessons from a middle level at-risk program. *The Clearing House*, 70 (Sept./Oct.): 48–51.

Weissberg, R. P., Walberg, H. J., O'Brien, M. U., and Kuster, C. B. (Eds.). (2003). *Long-Term Trends in the Well-Being of Children and Youth*. Washington, DC: Child Welfare League of America Press.

Wetzel, M. C. and McNaboe, K. A. (1997). Public and private partnerships in an alternative middle school program. *Preventing School Failure*, 41(4): 179–184.

White, B. and Madara, E. (eds.) (1992). *Self-Help Sourcebook . . . Finding and Forming Mutual Aid Self-Help Groups*, 4th ed. Denville, NJ: St. Clares-Riverside Medical Center.

Whitfield, C. (1984). *Healing the Child Within*. Deerfield Beach, FL: Health Communications, Inc.

Whitfield, C. (1990). *A Gift To Myself*. Deerfield Beach, FL: Health Communications, Inc.

Whitfield, C. (1991). *Co-Dependence: Healing The Human Condition*. Deerfield Beach, FL: Health Communications, Inc.

Widom, C. S. (2000). *The Cycle of Violence*. Available on-line. Washington, DC: U.S. Department of Justice, National Institute of Justice.

Widom, C.S. (1992). *The Cycle of Violence*. Washington, DC: National Institute of Justice.

Wiest, D.J., Wong, E.H., Cervantes, J.M., Craik, L., & Kreil, D.A. (2001). Intrinsic motivation among regular, special, and alternative education high school students. *Adolescence*, 36(141): 111–127.

Williams, K. (2002). Determining the effectiveness of anger management training and curricular infusion at an alternative school for students expelled for weapons. *Urban Education*, 37(1): 59–76.

Woititz, J. (1989). *Healing Your Sexual Self*. Deerfield Beach, FL: Health Communications, Inc.

Wolfe, L. (1991). *Women, Work, and School: Occupational Segregation and the Role of Education*. Boulder, CO: Westview Press.

Worrell, F. C. (1997). Predicting successful or non-successful at-risk status using demographic risk factors. *High School Journal*, 81(1): 46–54.

Index

About the Author

ANTHONY DALLMANN-JONES, Ph.D., founder and director of the National At-Risk Education Network (NAREN), has been a well-known advocate for at-risk youth and their educators for many years. He discovered an absence of an effective voice and organized support system to address perspectives on the critical issues in at-risk education that both students and educators must face on a daily basis. Society and even many school systems generally appear to be in denial or confused and frustrated about the best action steps to take. Meanwhile, the at-risk youth and the educators who care about them are frequently misunderstood and isolated. It is from these roots that Dr. Dallmann-Jones began formalizing his research into a quest for clarity and answers. From this he originated the name Shadow Children as a synonym for at-risk children. He also formed his ARME (or "At-Risk Mindful Educator") website and newsgroup in 1997 for his own graduate students, many of whom were teachers concerned about at-risk youth. Once the website and listserv became part of the web, teachers from all over the country asked to be part of the mailing list until it grew into the organization it is now, with a mailing list of over 65,000 educators! From these roots, NAREN came to fruition.

Dr. Dallmann-Jones, a graduate of Florida State University, was born into extreme poverty in Mobile, Alabama, and experienced first hand the impact of being raised in a dysfunctional family. He began teaching in 1965 in the small rural Ohio town of Spencerville. Since then he has taught in middle schools, high schools, colleges, and medium-security prisons. He was a central office educational administrator in

Jacksonville, Florida, and a Title III project director on Lookout Mountain, Tennessee.

Dr. Dallmann-Jones helped design the first accredited At-Risk master's degree program in the United States, which now graduate an average of 20 teachers a year specializing in working with at-risk youth. He has worked on behalf of at-risk "street children" with the Police Athletic League, in halfway houses, as a psychotherapist, and on three different Native American reservations.

Dr. Dallmann-Jones has published several books and videos, including:

- Crabapple—A True Story of Hope & Miracles
- Resolving Unifinished Business: Assessing the Effects of Being Raised in a Dysfunctional Environment
- The Expert Educator: A Reference Manual of Teaching Strategies for Quality Education
- The Handbook of Effective Teaching and Assessment Strategies
- Is Education Having a Heart Attack?

Dr. Dallmann-Jones is currently a graduate professor of educational psychology at Marian College. He speaks nationwide in schools, to civic groups, and at conventions on both at-risk education topics and teacher rejuvenation issues.

Contact Dr. Dallmann-Jones: asdjones@gmail.com
Anthony Dallmann-Jones, PhD
107½ State Street, Ste 5
Madison, WI 53703